The Reading Terminal
Market Cookbook

Netsi,

FEB. 24, 2002

The more I am gone from you,
The more I realize what's' really
important in my life – you!

Jimmy

XXOOXX

The Reading Terminal Market Cookbook

Ann Hazan & Irina Smith

CAMINO BOOKS, INC.
PHILADELPHIA

Manufactured in the United States of America

2 3 4 5 04 03 02 01

Library of Congress Cataloging-in-Publication Data

Hazan, Ann, 1946–
The Reading Terminal Market cookbook / by Ann Hazan & Irina Smith.
  p. cm.
  Includes index.
  ISBN 0-940159-33-3 (trade paper : alk. paper)
  1. Cookery, American. 2. Cookery—Pennsylvania—Philadelphia.
3. Reading Terminal Market (Philadelphia, Pa.)
I. Smith, Irina, 1942– . II. Reading Terminal Market (Philadelphia, Pa.)
III. Title.
TX715.H3954 1997
641.5973–dc21

96-47964

Line Art and Cover: Rhona Candeloro
Interior Design: Rick Ward

Reading Terminal Market® is a registered trademark of Reading Company. The trademark is
used under license with permission of Reading Company.

For information write:

Publisher
Camino Books, Inc.
P.O. Box 59026
Philadelphia, PA 19102

www.caminobooks.com

Acknowledgments

We truly love the Market and its people. Writing this book was a memorable experience for us. However, we know that it was only made possible with the cooperation, help and support of others. We wish to especially thank:

Ken Bookman, our editor—for working side by side with us and spending endless hours helping to polish the manuscript.

Edward Jutkowitz, our publisher—for seeing, as we did, the importance of keeping the Reading Terminal Market and its history alive through this cookbook and for his fortitude in working with us through three cookbooks.

Nancy Love, our agent—for sharing our feelings about the Market and for believing in the project and in us from the beginning.

Merchants of the Market, one and all—for putting up with our endless quest for information and for taking the time to talk to us. Also for your faith in the Market's survival throughout the years and for sharing your recipes, which we had much fun in testing.

Market customers—for sharing your recipes and for your loyalty and support in keeping the Market's image alive and active for the people of the city.

David O'Neil, past General Manager of the Market—for shaping the Market into what it is today. It would not have been possible without your vision and tenacity. A special thank you also, for your generosity in supplying many of the photographs used in this book.

Marcene Rogovin, current General Manager of the Market—for your advice and patience in supplying us with market information.

Duane Perry, from the Reading Terminal Market—for your interest and support in this project.

Our husbands—for willingly offering to taste the recipes we tested and for your patience and encouragement throughout.

Contents

Introduction

The money that "Philbert" collects benefits food and education programs in needy communities.

hiladelphia's Reading Terminal Market opened on February 22, 1892, and it was quickly recognized as one of the world's great food markets. More than a century later, it still is.

Reading Terminal Market is a traditional stall market. Its approximately 80 merchants represent a wide variety of ethnic backgrounds and Philadelphia neighborhoods. Some of the merchants sell meats, poultry, fish, produce, and groceries, while others sell prepared foods to eat in or take out. Where else can you find a Lebanese immigrant frying falafel, a Korean artistically arranging fruits and vegetables, a Japanese preparing sushi, a Pennsylvania Dutch farmer displaying a traditional favorite like shoofly pie, women in pinafores with traditional white head caps rolling and twisting the ever-popular soft pretzel, or, for that matter, an African-American at a Sicilian sandwich stand slicing imported prosciutto – all under one roof? Nowhere else.

Today, Reading Terminal Market attracts 80,000 customers a week and is the food destination of choice for Philadelphians who live and work in the city, as

The merchants of the Reading Terminal Market in the 1970s.

Patrons enjoy their meals at a restaurant located on the Filbert Street side of the market, circa 1910.

well as for many suburbanites. It's situated in Center City between Arch and Filbert Streets and between 11th and 12th Streets – close to trains, buses, downtown department stores, hotels, offices, and the city's Chinatown section. In 1994, the market got a new neighbor, the mammoth Pennsylvania Convention Center across Arch Street, and almost overnight the market's customer base grew dramatically with conventioneers and out-of-towners joining the locals who already were drawn to this splendidly preserved historic resource, which is listed in the National Register of Historic Places.

Hundreds flock to the market to enjoy breakfast, lunch, or early dinner. At lunchtime especially, the counters and seating areas fill up with hungry patrons from all walks of life – lawyers, politicians, priests, and construction workers. Frequently at midday, a local band or a musician is providing entertainment, and a piano is ready for any aspiring pianist who wants to entertain the crowd. The market is renowned for its Amish and Mennonite farmers and merchants who bring meats, poultry, game, and produce from their farms, many of these Pennsylvania Dutch coming from nearby Lancaster County. Indeed, the market is known for the availability of many Philadelphia specialties and Pennsylvania products.

In addition to being a food emporium, the market boasts several cookware and kitchen shops, a well-stocked cookbook stall, newspaper and magazine stands, several craft shops featuring the clothing and jewelry of local artisans, flower shops, and even a shoeshine stand against a backdrop of a mural depicting the signing of the Declaration of Independence.

Felix Spatola and Sons offered wholesale produce at the market from the 1920s until the early 1960s.

The market's history goes back to the original open-air markets set up on the banks of the Delaware River in the late 1600s. These markets later moved to an arcade in the center of what was then known as High Street (now Market Street). As the city developed, these markets moved even farther west, to between 11th and 12th Streets. By the 19th century, they were referred to as the Franklin and Farmer's Markets.

When the Reading Railroad was looking for a site for its proposed Reading Terminal, it negotiated for the site of the markets by offering to build merchants a new indoor facility as part of the train complex. They built the train shed, a grand headhouse at 12th and Market, as well as a food market that was unrivaled in America.

Reading Terminal Market became the center for food distribution for the city. Foods could now easily be shipped in by train. Beneath the market floor was a massive cold-storage area – about 500,000 cubic feet of space divided into rooms of varying temperatures for properly storing different meats, poultry, fruits, and vegetables. The market also provided ice to merchants and ice for the railroad's passenger cars, dining facilities, and refrigerated express cars.

Many of the longstanding market merchants remember being told of how carriages of the wealthy would line up on 12th Street while the chefs shopped for their employers. These same merchants also recalled the hard times – the two world wars, the Depression, food rationing, and food stamps. They recall the impact of these events on themselves and their families, businesses, and customers.

Those were days when the market was effective and well served the needs of Philadelphians. But after World War II, the market suffered a decline as mass-merchandising, fast food, and suburbanizing took ever greater hold in America. Food began to move by truck as more highways were built, and Reading Terminal Market's own food network began to deteriorate, as did the market's structure and appearance. By the 1970s, the market was in serious trouble and was showing signs of ruin and decay. By the time the last train rolled out of Reading Terminal in the 1980s, the market's fortunes were looking bleak.

To help stimulate business in the early 1980s, the Reading Company made major renovations and worked to increase the numbers of eat-in and take-out food stands.

David O'Neil, who became the market's new general manager in 1981, played a pivotal role in its resurgence. In addition to recruiting new eateries and other interesting merchants, he went out to Lancaster County, an hour's drive but a world away, and persuaded many Amish and Mennonite farmers to establish a Pennsylvania Dutch section of the market. It would become one of the market's major attractions. Some of the vendors would sell not just prepared foods but the ingredients for their specialties.

Customers choose the perfect cut of meat at the Terminal Dressed Beef Co. in the late 1940s.

O'Neil was sustained partly by his own boyhood experiences at the market and his growing love for the place. "It's a throwback," he said, "where people used to fast food can experience what it was like before America was gobbled up by chains. Here you can get the ethnic diversity of Philadelphia and all the neighborhoods. You come here and people say 'Hi, how are you?' You know the meat man. I think in a city, people really crave human contact – and they get it at the market."

Many of the market's founding merchants stayed on during the tough times, loyal to the market and nurturing faith that it would return to its grander times. The market was, in fact, coming back.

Its brush with disaster might explain the fear that surrounded the next critical period in Reading Terminal Market's tumultuous history. The planning and construction of a convention center across from the market on Arch Street had merchants and shoppers fearing for the market's survival as a true farmers' market. Locals feared a change in the nature of the merchants. Would the market become a souvenir trap? Would it discourage and chase away loyal customers? Or would it be torn down and destroyed altogether as a huge convention center went up? "Save the Market" buttons began popping up everywhere, and thousands signed petitions urging the preservation of this city treasure.

Customers line up to buy meats from Florence Yeager (wearing turban) and her family in the early 1940s. C.M. Yeager and Co. was located across from the Terminal Dressed Beef Company.

Florence Yeager entertains the crowd during Spring Festival at the market, circa 1960. Although she took over her father's meat business, she was also an accomplished opera singer and artist.

The fears did not materialize. Change did, but the market came through. Despite considerable acrimony, the Reading Terminal Market Merchants' Association worked with the Pennsylvania Convention Center Authority. The Reading Railroad supported the market in the 1890s, and now the Convention Center Authority was supporting it in the 1990s. Renovations were desperately needed, and they were made, though not without great pain to the merchants and shoppers. During the renovation, one section of the market at a time was closed off, with every merchant enduring one temporary relocation. But the market remained open during the renovation period. When it was done, the structure and its supporting electrical, plumbing, and air-conditioning systems were improved, and the market got the new roof it so badly needed.

Now, the market is cleaner, brighter, and cooler in summer. The longstanding merchants are still around – and so are their longtime customers. Once again the market was thrown into turmoil, once again it survived. The market continues to serve the entire community and region in its historic setting.

The Reading Terminal Market Corporation assumed management responsibility for the market in September 1995, a 29-year commitment to preserve the historic mission of the market as a shopping destination for the widest range of locally grown and produced food. Marcene Rogovin, the market's current general manager, says "It remains the one place where people from every neighborhood and background come together to promote rural-urban links and to highlight the culture and heritage of the region's farming community." In addition to handling the day-to-day details of managing the market, Rogovin is developing strategies to maintain the market's personality and to ensure its success into the 21st century. Included are plans for a demonstration kitchen that will serve as a resource for nutrition education, cooking demonstrations, and seasonal festivals, all featuring market merchants.

Two major organizations were established to strengthen the market's influence in the community. The Reading Terminal Farmers' Market Trust was created by market merchants in 1991 to support the establishment of stable sources of good-quality, fresh, affordable foods in underserved communities and to strengthen the connection between farmers and consumers. The trust is a charitable organization and operates Community Farmers' Markets in partnership with communities throughout the city. In 1993, the Reading Terminal Market Merchants' Catering Company was formed to cater special events in the market and elsewhere using foods supplied and prepared by market merchants.

Farmers' markets in this country have taken on a new ambiance. Homegrown and organic farming has gained a new popularity and growing respect. Although farmers' markets are not new to the Philadelphia region or, for that matter, to the world, fresh foods have become very important to Americans, and markets are adapting to this trend. These are the places where you can find seasonal products, homemade vinegars, homebaked breads, and local honeys – and where you meet the farmer or producer. It has become a way of life for many people, and we've found that Reading Terminal Market has also adjusted to the change in times.

Mastering the intricacies of selling in farmers' markets around the world can be fascinating, challenging, and at times frustrating. Most merchants are proud people and often display a refined sense of artistry. They painstakingly arrange fruits and vegetables in attractive, orderly displays, and the butcher and poultryman will take the time to describe a certain cut of meat or to give out recipes for preparation.

Markets in Philadelphia have provided an incentive for cooking for centuries. Another Philadelphia attraction – and a competitor of the Reading Terminal Market – is the historic Italian Market, located on Ninth Street in South Philadelphia. And there are other farmers' markets nearby, including those in Chestnut Hill, Germantown, Manayunk, and West Philadelphia. There are farmers' and public markets across the nation – New York's market at Union Square, the Fulton Fish Market, and the Bronx Terminal Market; Baltimore's Lexington Market and Broadway Market; Seattle's Pike Place Market. And there are renowned food markets overseas, in Paris, London, Venice, and Prague, and in the Far East from Hong Kong to Beijing, Delhi and Bombay, all offering unforgettable experiences, and all expressing their unique culture and foods.

But you don't have to travel that far, for Philadelphia's Reading Terminal Market catches the essence of many flavors from around the world and is considered by many to be the best in the country.

We can attest to Reading Terminal Market's outstanding qualities because for more than 20 years, we have enjoyed it and basked in what it has to offer.

Shopping and spending time in farmers' markets was not a new experience for us. As youngsters, our parents would take us along to the neighborhood markets wherever we lived at the time. And as we grew older and traveled on our own to even more cities around the world, we were still drawn to the markets, out of curiosity and interest. Many of the markets were charming in their own right, and we were pleased to see them bustling with activity. But we both agreed: There was no place like home, meaning our very own Reading Terminal Market. It is truly our second home, especially after years of researching and writing this cookbook, which we hope is a tribute to its greatness. We especially love chatting with merchants and customers. The market atmosphere lends itself to really getting to know its people, the people we call the market family.

We enjoyed hearing the story from one loyal customer who recalled how she came to shop at the market. One day, her cat ate the veal chop that her mother-in-law put out for dinner, so she went to the market to buy another chop. The woman who waited on her was so bubbly and friendly that the customer ended up telling her the circumstances of her purchase. They both had a good laugh. The customer was so impressed with how accommodating the merchant was that she went back time and time again. She still shops there after 20 years. We love the story, for we believe it captures the warmth of the market, the friendly, more-than-willing-to-help-you place to shop.

The market is never more wonderful and alive than during the holiday seasons. We can't wait for each new season to arrive with its bounty of holiday foods and seasonal fruits and vegetables, to see customers selecting their turkey or duck for holiday dinner, to see the stalls decorated for Christmas, to see the first pussy willows and tulips at the flower stands and know that spring is just around the corner, or to feast on crabs and homegrown corn all summer long.

The market features many special annual festivals throughout the year, such as the Lobster Festival, the Maple Syrup Festival, the Strawberry Festival, and Pennsylvania Dutch Day. A popular Philadelphia yearly tradition is a fundraiser called the Valentine to the Market. All are well attended, and we're only two of the thousands of people who have come to eagerly anticipate those events.

Over the years, we have conducted cooking demonstrations for many of these festivals and, in addition, have brought groups of students and tourists to introduce them to the market and what it has to offer. The market is a place where we bring our friends and family and spend some of the most enjoyable times together. Whether we eat there or shop for food to prepare at home, we feel we are getting the best there is.

This cookbook is a celebration of Reading Terminal Market and is meant to open your eyes to the many wonders of a great Philadelphia tradition. Philadelphians who live in the city enjoy walking to the market to shop and to talk to their many merchant friends. The market also offers ready access to virtually all of the area's mass transportation, so people who live outside Center City can shop in their favorite place as well. Business people enjoy taking a break and lunching at their favorite counter. Every day, conventioneers are discovering this exciting bazaar of new and old merchants, and browsing tourists are surprised at the liveliness of this turn-of-the-century market.

More than simply guiding you through this remarkable place, we hope that this book will introduce you to a new way of enjoying that Saturday morning, that weekday lunch break, that brief respite before the train home, or, together with special recipes from your favorite merchants, that dinner at home. We know you will delight in the market's diversity and timeless grace.

Finally, we would each like to add a favorite recipe to the collection that follows. As you may have guessed, we make these from foods we buy at Reading Terminal Market.

ANN HAZAN'S ROAST LEG OF LAMB WITH ORZO

This Greek dish is prepared for a traditional Easter dinner using the spring lamb available at the market during this season. Orzo, which looks like long-grain rice, is actually a pasta made from semolina. It is excellent served with a sprinkling of freshly grated cheese alongside roasted lamb or chicken.

1 leg of lamb, $3^1/_2$ to 4 pounds

2 large cloves garlic, peeled and sliced in half

1 medium onion, thinly sliced

2 tablespoons olive oil

2 tablespoons unsalted butter

1 tablespoon oregano

Salt and freshly ground pepper to taste

2 cups canned Italian plum tomatoes, drained and chopped

$^1/_2$ cup water

$3^1/_2$ cups chicken stock

$1^1/_2$ cups orzo

Freshly grated Locatelli Romano cheese

Preheat oven to 350° F. Make four 1-inch cuts in the lamb, and insert the garlic slivers into the cuts. Place lamb in a roasting pan and spread the onion around the lamb.

In a small saucepan, heat the oil and butter together, and pour over the lamb. Season with oregano, salt, and pepper. Place in the oven, and cook for 10 to 15 minutes. Add the tomato and water, and continue cooking for approximately $1^1/_2$ to 2 hours, basting frequently with pan juices. During cooking, add more water to pan juices if necessary. A meat thermometer inserted into the thickest part of the meat should register 140° F. for rare, 160° for medium. Remove lamb, cover loosely with foil, and keep warm.

Add the chicken stock to the roasting pan, stir in the orzo, return to the oven, and cook for approximately 30 to 40 minutes, or until the orzo is cooked and the liquid is absorbed. Slice the lamb and serve with the orzo, topped with a sprinkling of the grated cheese.

Makes 4 servings

IRINA SMITH'S PORK LOIN WITH LEMONGRASS AND SOY SAUCE

An interesting ingredient in this dish is lemongrass, once hard to find but now readily available and used as a flavoring to accent sauces, soups, and marinades. The lemongrass is sliced very thin, then chopped before being added to other ingredients.

1 pork loin, $3^1/_2$ to 4 pounds

$^1/_4$ cup soy sauce

1 tablespoon lemon juice

1 tablespoon honey

2 tablespoons chopped lemongrass

3 cloves garlic, chopped

$^1/_2$ tablespoon chopped fresh ginger

$1^1/_2$ cups chicken stock

Zest of 1 lemon

1 red pepper, thinly sliced

1 scallion, chopped

$^1/_2$ cup water chestnuts, sliced

$1^1/_2$ tablespoons cornstarch

1 teaspoon sesame oil

Place pork in a shallow pan. In a bowl, combine soy sauce, lemon juice, honey, lemongrass, half the garlic, and ginger. Pour over pork and refrigerate for 4 to 6 hours. Remove 30 minutes before cooking.

Preheat oven to 350° F. Remove pork from marinade and place in a roasting pan. Pour a little of the marinade over the pork, and roast for approximately 2 hours. Add remaining marinade and cook another 15 to 20 minutes, or until pork is cooked through. Remove pork and keep warm.

To the pan juices, add $^1/_4$ cup of the chicken stock, lemon zest, red pepper, scallion, water chestnuts, and remaining garlic, and cook about 5 minutes. Mix cornstarch into remaining chicken stock and stir into sauce. Add sesame oil and cook until sauce is slightly thickened. Slice the pork and serve with the sauce on the side.

Makes 6 servings

CHAPTER 1 .... *The Longtime Market Families*

Margerum's Old Fashion Corner

Not only is Margerum's Old Fashion Corner one of the oldest businesses in Reading Terminal Market, but to this day it's one of the best reflections of the market's atmosphere, retaining the look, feel, and many of the artifacts from a century ago.

William B. Margerum opened the store in 1902, and at the time it occupied about a quarter of the market's space. Originally, the store sold meats, produce, beans, and grains, and Margerum's customers soon referred to his store as the "House of Excellence." Margerum, with a large fleet of cars, would deliver to customers outside Philadelphia.

Noelle Margerum took over the business in the late 1970s, and she represents the fourth generation of her family to run the store. Today, Margerum's no longer sells meats or produce, but the shelves are packed with an amazing variety of canned, bottled, and dried goods. Among Margerum's best sellers are the many varieties of beans and grains that are displayed in replicas of the original bins in the front of the store.

William B. Margerum (right with moustache) offers a variety of products including poultry, meat, and butter.

"The great-granddaughter of the man who built the original bins continued to shop here for years," Noelle Margerum boasted proudly. "There are not only generations of shop owners at the market, but generations of shoppers as well. This is truly an old-fashioned store. We usually have that 'something' that is hard to find anyplace else," she said, pointing out such items as barley malt and Lyle's Golden Syrup, which is used in many English baking recipes. Noelle and her sister Carol are great gardeners, and they bring in many of their organically grown herbs. One favorite is licorice cinnamon basil, and a regular customer frequently calls for fresh lavender to use in her scone recipe.

Margerum's still uses the original machine to grind nuts for cashew butter, and customers frequently request natural, old-style, freshly ground peanut butter as well as poppy-seed butter, which is made in yet another grinding machine.

SUN-DRIED TOMATO TORTA

The ingredients for this tasty appetizer come from Noelle Margerum. It's easily put together and can be made two or three days ahead. Toss any leftovers on hot pasta. Sun-dried tomatoes can be bought already packed in oil, but if you want to make them yourself, cut plum tomatoes in half, place them on a baking tray, and roast them in a 150° to 200° F. oven for 6 to 8 hours, or until they turn dark red and are shriveled slightly. They can then be preserved in olive oil.

8 ounces cream cheese

$\frac{1}{4}$ pound (1 stick) unsalted butter, at room temperature, cut in pieces

1 clove garlic, cut in large pieces

1 cup freshly grated Parmesan cheese

$\frac{1}{2}$ cup sun-dried tomatoes in oil,

drained and chopped, oil reserved

2 cups tightly packed fresh basil leaves, for garnish

3 sun-dried tomatoes, thinly sliced, for garnish

Crackers or toasted sliced Italian bread

In a blender or food processor, mix cream cheese, butter, garlic, and Parmesan cheese until smooth. Remove half the cheese mixture and place in a bowl. Add the $\frac{1}{2}$ cup sun-dried tomatoes and 1 tablespoon of the reserved tomato oil to the remaining cheese mixture. Blend until smooth. Scrape the mixture into the reserved cheese, and mix with a fork until blended. Cover and refrigerate 20 minutes, or until firm enough to shape.

On a platter, form the cheese into a mound, smoothing it with a spatula. Cover with an inverted bowl (do not use plastic wrap because it will stick to cheese) and chill 2 to 3 hours. Remove bowl and bring cheese to room temperature. Arrange basil leaves and sun-dried tomato slices around the cheese, and serve with crackers or bread slices.

Makes 8 servings

BLACK BEAN POT

From Noelle Margerum's selection of dried beans comes this heartwarming winter bean dish. It freezes well, so make it in large batches. Black beans, sometimes called turtle beans, are oval with black skins and are rich in taste. In addition to going well in soups and stews, they are a colorful attraction in vegetable salads. Pinto beans are medium-sized with beige and brown speckles and are popular in many Tex-Mex and Mexican dishes. Kidney beans are red or white. The white ones are sometimes called cannellini. The red beans are most often used in chilis, while the white beans are popular in Italian dishes.

$^1/_2$ pound dried black beans	2 bay leaves
$^1/_4$ pound dried pinto beans	1 teaspoon salt
$^1/_4$ pound dried kidney beans	2 tablespoons molasses
3 tablespoons olive oil	2 tablespoons honey
1 small onion, chopped	$^1/_4$ cup packed brown sugar
2 cloves garlic, minced	$^1/_4$ cup dark rum
1 rib celery, chopped	2 teaspoons dry mustard
1 carrot, chopped	1 teaspoon dried thyme
6 cups water	2 tablespoons butter or margarine

Rinse beans thoroughly, sorting through and removing any debris. Place beans in a large saucepan, add water to cover, and set aside for 2 to 3 hours. Drain.

Heat the oil in a medium skillet over medium heat. Sauté the onion, garlic, celery, and carrot in the hot oil until the onion is tender but not browned, about 2 minutes. Transfer mixture into the beans, and add the 6 cups of water, bay leaves, and salt. Place saucepan over medium heat and bring to a boil. Reduce heat, cover, and simmer until beans are almost tender, about $1^1/_2$ hours. During cooking, add more hot water as needed to keep beans covered.

Drain beans, reserving cooking liquid. Remove bay leaves. Preheat oven to 300° F. In a bowl, combine molasses, honey, brown sugar, 2 tablespoons of the rum, dry mustard, and thyme, and mix well.

Place beans in an ovenproof casserole and stir in the molasses mixture. Add enough reserved cooking liquid to just cover beans. Place lid on saucepan and bake for 1 hour. Uncover, dot with butter or margarine, and bake an additional 20 minutes. Stir in remaining rum just before serving.

Makes 6 to 8 servings

◆

HERB VINEGAR MARINADE

Noelle Margerum makes and sells many herb vinegars.

$^2/_3$ cup olive oil

$^1/_3$ cup herb vinegar (any variety)

1 clove garlic, minced

$^1/_2$ teaspoon salt

$^1/_4$ teaspoon freshly ground black or white pepper

$^1/_2$ teaspoon thyme leaves

Combine all ingredients in a container. Cover and shake well. Chill for 4 hours. Pour over meat, poultry, or fish, and let marinate for 1 to 2 hours. Grill or broil.

Makes 1 cup

MARGERUM'S MARINADE FOR BEEF, LAMB, OR PORK

This marinade recipe has been in the Margerum family for five generations. Noelle Margerum's great-grandfather used to share it with many of his customers.

$\frac{1}{2}$ cup French dressing

$\frac{1}{2}$ cup Margerum's herb wine vinegar (or any variety)

Pinch of salt

Dash of ground pepper

Dash of hot pepper sauce

Pinch of dried thyme

Combine all ingredients. Use as a marinade for 2 to 3 pounds of beef, lamb, or pork. (Cover the meat in the marinade for 1 to 2 hours, and cook the meat under a broiler or over coals, basting frequently with marinade.)

Makes about 1 cup

Pearl's Oyster Bar

Today's patrons of Pearl's Oyster Bar may not know that the business originally occupied a far larger portion of Reading Terminal Market than it does now, along the market's 12th Street side. In fact, Pearl's was originally part of Margerum's Old Fashion Corner when that store was owned by William Margerum, great-grandfather of current owner Noelle Margerum.

Fresh fish was brought in daily and was displayed on one side of the aisle and beyond, along lunch counters, where customers would sit and consume large platters of fried fish and oysters. The Margerum family sold this part of the business to Vincent Cardello in the early 1930s, and it became Vincent's Seafood. Vincent Cardello (a spelling that no one could vouch for) was the longest-tenured owner of this unique place and during his ownership brought in live turtles so that he could prepare his snapper soup from scratch. In the late '40s, he sold to a woman named Pearl, who gave the business her own name, calling it Pearl's Oyster Bar. Although several of the market longtimers we asked remember Pearl as a warmhearted, friendly woman, none could remember her last name. Pearl installed the market's first lobster tanks, which remained until she sold to "Iggy" Reynolds, also known as "Ashes." In the early 1970s, Reynolds remodeled the portion along the 12th Street side, and there he moved Pearl's. He kept the name, and today's Pearl's Oyster Bar is as popular a spot in the market as it ever was.

Pearl's present owners, Lisa and Danny Braunstein, bought the business in 1981 and have continued serving the traditional seafood platters, prepared by Rob Swinton, their wonderful, cheerful cook, who has played an important role at Pearl's for many years. Rob started with "Iggy" Reynolds as a dishwasher at age 12 and, after graduating from Benjamin Franklin High School, worked full time in the kitchen under three different cooks. He learned some of his cooking skills with them, he said, but "I really learned to cook by being thrown into doing it myself."

He remembers the days when nothing was locked up, when everything was open, when everyone could be trusted. Now everything is kept under lock and key.

Swinton enjoys mingling with the customers, so "they can see me and I can see them," he said. Every day, many of those customers lunch at the black-and-white tiled counter, where they enjoy large platters of fried oysters, oyster stew, and countless other dishes in the best of Pearl's longstanding tradition of generous servings, a tradition that has remained the same through several ownerships.

PEARL'S FRIED OYSTERS

Rob Swinton, the chef at Pearl's Oyster Bar, prefers using bread crumbs for his fried oysters. He says they give a lighter coating than cracker crumbs.

Oil, for frying

Flour, for dusting

2 eggs

$\frac{1}{3}$ cup milk

Salt and freshly ground pepper to taste

2 cups bread crumbs

24 large oysters

Lemon wedges, for garnish

In a deep skillet or fryer, pour in enough oil to come halfway up the sides of the skillet. Heat oil until hot. (The oil is at the proper temperature when a bread cube sizzles on contact and browns in a few seconds.)

Meanwhile, place flour on a shallow plate. Whisk together the eggs, milk, salt, and pepper in a mixing bowl. Place bread crumbs on another shallow plate. Lightly flour the oysters, dip them into the egg mixture, then drain off excess batter. Coat with bread crumbs.

Fry the oysters until browned, turning them over once or twice during the cooking. Drain on paper towels, garnish with lemon slices, and serve.

Makes 4 servings

PEARL'S OYSTER STEW

A tip from Rob Swinton, the chef at Pearl's Oyster Bar, on making a good oyster stew: Cook the oysters and milk separately.

2 pints shucked medium oysters   1 tablespoon butter
6 cups milk   Paprika, for garnish

In a saucepan, gently cook the oysters in their juices until the edges are slightly curled, about 6 minutes. In another saucepan, heat the milk just to a boil, and gradually pour it over the oysters. Add the butter, and stir. Ladle into soup bowls, and sprinkle a bit of paprika on top of each serving.

Makes 4 servings

A.A. Halteman's Poultry

Halteman's Poultry has been in the market since 1943, and the stand should not be confused with Lester Halteman's in the adjacent aisle. "Sonny" Halteman took over from his father in 1960 and has seen many changes over the years. One that he remembered was that "my father only sold dressed chickens and eggs. In those days, customers wanted only whole chickens, not cut-up chickens like they do today."

He has also witnessed an expansion of the stand's offerings. Sonny realized when he took over the business from his father that the ways of eating and the things people wanted were changing, so he added lunch meats, sausages, and turkey products to the chickens, which were now cut-up and oven-ready. Many regular customers come by weekly, but Sonny said he also sees many new faces as people discover the market. Sonny finds that "turkey products, such as turkey jerky and 'turkeroni' sausage, have become popular with customers who don't want to eat pork."

MEXICAN TURKEY LASAGNA

"There are hundreds of ways to prepare chicken and turkey," Sonny said, "and everyone has a favorite way," so regardless of what part of the world you come from, the preparation of chicken or turkey reflects nationality by the use of different herbs and spices. This recipe from Sonny shows just that with its blending of Italian and Mexican ingredients.

1 pound ground turkey

8 ears fresh corn, shucked, or 1 19-ounce can whole corn, drained

1 15-ounce can tomato sauce, or homemade

1 cup picante sauce (available in jars at many markets), plus additional for serving

1 tablespoon chili powder

2 cloves garlic, crushed

8 ounces cottage cheese (any variety)

2 eggs, lightly beaten

$1/_4$ cup freshly grated Parmesan cheese

1 teaspoon dried oregano

1 teaspoon dried basil

Pinch salt

12 corn tortillas

1 cup (4 ounces) shredded Cheddar cheese

Preheat oven to 375° F. In a nonstick skillet, brown the turkey and drain any fat that has accumulated in the skillet. Add the corn, tomato sauce, picante sauce, chili powder, and garlic, and combine. Simmer over low heat for about 5 minutes, stirring frequently, and set aside.

In a bowl, combine the cottage cheese, eggs, Parmesan cheese, oregano, basil, and salt. Mix well.

Grease a 13 x 9 x 2-inch baking dish and arrange 6 of the tortillas on the bottom and sides, overlapping as necessary. Top with half the meat mixture, then spoon the cheese mixture over the meat. Arrange the remaining tortillas over the cheese, and top with the remaining meat mixture.

Bake for about 30 minutes, or until hot and bubbly. Remove, and sprinkle with the shredded Cheddar cheese. Let stand for 10 minutes before serving. Serve with additional picante sauce on the side.

Makes 8 servings

CURRIED TURKEY AND RICE

Sonny Halteman gave us this excellent ground-turkey recipe, which uses curry powder. Curry powder is a subtle blend of spices and usually includes coriander, cumin, turmeric, mustard, fenugreek, red chili, and black pepper.

1 1/2 pounds ground turkey	1/2 teaspoon salt
1 medium onion, sliced	2 cloves garlic, minced
1 1/2 cups long-grain rice, uncooked	1/4 teaspoon ground ginger
	1/4 teaspoon ground cinnamon
3 cups water	2 tablespoons peanut butter
1 cube chicken bouillon	1 teaspoon honey
1 tablespoon curry powder	1/2 cup raisins

Cook the turkey and onion in a large skillet over medium heat, stirring until the turkey is lightly browned. Drain any fat that may have accumulated.

Add the remaining ingredients, bring to a boil, reduce heat to a simmer, cover, and cook about 25 minutes, stirring occasionally until the rice is tender and the liquid has been absorbed. If necessary, add small amounts of hot water.

Makes 6 servings

◆

L. Halteman Family Country Foods

Melvin C. Halteman opened his business and established a stall at Reading Terminal Market in 1918. In 1958, his son and daughter-in-law, Lester and Millie, took over the family business. Lester remembers his parents bringing him to the market as a child and added, "The market back then acted like a child-care center to many of the merchants' children."

The Haltemans are struck by the general resurgence of interest in shopping at farmers' markets. "People like the personalized service they get here and tell us they feel part of the family, like one of my father-in-law's customers who is now 95 years old and continues to shop here each week for her chickens and home-grown vegetables that she cooks herself," said Millie Halteman.

From their 75-acre farm in northern Montgomery County, outside Philadelphia, the Haltemans bring in home-raised poultry, ducks, geese, and rabbits, and are one of only a few sources in the city for home-smoked oxtail and beef bacon. Lines are long during the holiday season with customers ordering and picking up their fresh turkeys. The Haltemans also grow and sell seasonal fruits and vegetables, which are colorfully displayed, as well as herbs and potted plants ready for spring planting.

Rows of jellies, relishes, and pickles, all made by Millie Halteman's Aunt Anna Rieser, are lined up on the countertops. A local beekeeper supplies wildflower, clover, alfalfa, and goldenrod honeys.

Unusual seasonal fruits are often found nestling among their vegetables—fruits such as ground cherries that are available only during August "and make a wonderful, scrumptious pie," Millie Halteman says enthusiastically.

ROAST MUSCOVY DUCK WITH SAUERKRAUT AND HERBS

Millie Halteman gave us this Pennsylvania Dutch recipe that has been in her family for generations. Sauerkraut complements the richness of the bird and is often used in cooking game dishes. If there is a hunter in the family, wild duck is excellent prepared this way.

1 Muscovy duck, 4 to 5 pounds	1 teaspoon dried sage
1 teaspoon dried oregano	2 pounds sauerkraut, drained and rinsed
1 teaspoon dried marjoram	

Preheat oven to 350° F. Thoroughly rinse the duck inside and out, and pat it dry. Remove excess fat from the cavity. Season the duck with the oregano, marjoram, and sage, and stuff it with as much of the sauerkraut as will comfortably fill the cavity. Tie the legs together with string.

Add the remaining sauerkraut to the bottom of the roasting pan, and place the duck on top. Cover and roast until done, approximately 2½ hours. To test the duck for tenderness, wiggle the legs back and forth; if they move easily, the duck is fully cooked.

Remove the duck from the oven, let stand for a few minutes, then carve into slices and serve with the sauerkraut.

Makes 4 servings

CHOW CHOW

Chow chow is a popular Pennsylvania Dutch relish. We obtained this version from Millie Halteman's Aunt Anna Rieser, who makes many of the relishes and preserves that Halteman sells. The sweet and sour flavor should be to your taste, so alter the amounts of sugar and vinegar accordingly.

4 cups small pickles

4 cups green or yellow beans, trimmed and cut into 1-inch pieces

4 cups lima beans

4 cups fresh corn kernels

2 cups celery, cut into $\frac{1}{2}$-inch pieces

2 green peppers, chopped

2 cups chopped red pepper

1 cup chopped yellow pepper

1 cup small white onions, peeled

1 tablespoon dry mustard

$1\frac{1}{2}$ cups sugar

$3\frac{1}{2}$ cups white wine or cider vinegar

Cook each of the vegetables separately until tender, but not soft. Drain and place in a large bowl. In a large saucepan, combine the mustard, sugar, and vinegar, and bring to a boil, stirring until the sugar has dissolved. Add the vegetables to the hot liquid, bring back to a boil, and simmer for 1 to 2 minutes. Ladle into hot, sterilized jars and seal according to manufacturer's directions.

Makes approximately 10 pints

SOUR CHERRY PIE

When local sour cherries are in season, this is a juicy, delicious pie to make. Watch for sour cherries from Lester Halteman's; they're quite tart but they mellow during cooking. Millie Halteman said you can also prepare this pie by using regular cherries.

Crust for 8-inch pie, from standard recipe or storebought

5 ounces chopped walnuts, finely chopped

1 cup sugar

4 tablespoons butter, softened

2 tablespoons flour

2 eggs, lightly beaten

2 tablespoons quick-cooking tapioca

4 cups pitted cherries

Preheat oven to 350° F. Line an 8-inch pie plate with the pastry. In a medium bowl, combine the walnuts, half the sugar, butter, 1 tablespoon of the flour, and the eggs, and mix just until blended. The mixture will be slightly sticky.

Pit the cherries over a bowl in which the juices can collect. To the juices, add the remaining flour, tapioca, and remaining sugar. Stir, then let sit for about 10 minutes until the flour and tapioca have been absorbed in the juices.

Pour the cherry mixture into the crust, and spoon the crumb topping over cherries. Bake for about 45 minutes, or until the crust is lightly browned. Let cool and serve.

Makes 6 servings

Godshall's Poultry

The Godshalls keep up with modern times and show their creativity by taking such traditional cuts of meat as cutlets, chops, scallopine, and London broil and making those cuts available to their customers by substituting turkey and chicken products. Godshall's will do other things with its poultry, too: Steve Frankenfield, a current owner, will bone a turkey leg and turn it into a delicious piece of dark meat, suitable for stuffing. He keeps a good stock of smoked turkey sausage and turkey kielbasa sausages, all bountifully displayed behind glass-encased counters.

Ernst and Eva Godshall have run the Godshall poultry business in the market since 1935. Eva, the sister of neighboring stall owner Lester Halteman, worked for Ernst's father before marrying Ernst, who said, with a twinkle in his eye, "She never lost her job."

They recall the early days when C.K. Godshall started the business in 1916, and described how his father collected poultry from local farmers and dressed the poultry before bringing it to the market to sell. In those days, most customers prepared only whole poultry, but Godshall's always had chicken parts available as well. Like many other longtime market denizens, Ernst recalled two defining

C.K. Godshall, Ernie Godshall's father, manning his grocery stand.

eras in the market's history – the Depression and the war years – and how the loyalty of Philadelphians who continued to shop regularly at the market helped their business survive. The business today is still in the family. Julie, a niece, and her husband, Steve Frankenfield, bought Godshall's in 1985 and have continued the family tradition of selling organically raised poultry, quail, and Cornish game hens. Although they're now retired, Ernst and Eva can still be seen working at the stand, side by side, on Fridays and Saturdays.

ROAST QUAIL WITH PORT SAUCE

For a delicious change of pace, try this recipe from the Frankenfields, today's owners of Godshall's. It uses a wonderful combination of figs, orange juice, and Port wine.

Port sauce:

1 cup port wine

$1/2$ cup orange juice

3 tablespoons lemon juice

1 shallot, finely chopped

$1/2$ clove garlic, minced

$1/4$ teaspoon dried thyme

1 dried fig, chopped

Stuffing:

6 slices bacon, diced

1 small onion, chopped

1 clove garlic, minced

$1/4$ cup port wine

2 dried figs, chopped

$1/3$ cup fresh bread crumbs

Salt and freshly ground pepper to taste

Quail:

8 whole quail, boned if desired

$1/4$ teaspoon salt

1 tablespoon garlic powder

1 tablespoon black pepper

1 teaspoon cayenne pepper

1 teaspoon paprika

8 bacon slices

To make the sauce, place the wine, orange juice, lemon juice, shallot, garlic, and thyme in a small saucepan and bring to a boil. Continue boiling until reduced by half and somewhat thickened, about 10 minutes. Add the chopped fig, return mixture to a boil, reduce heat, and let simmer for 1 minute. Cool and refrigerate until needed.

To make the stuffing, sauté the bacon until lightly browned in a large skillet over medium heat. Do not overcook. Reduce heat to low, add the onion and garlic, and cook until onion is translucent, about 10 minutes. Add wine and figs, increase heat, bring mixture to a low boil, and cook for 2 to 3 minutes. Add bread crumbs, mix well, and season with salt and pepper. Set aside.

Preheat oven to 375° F. Fill each quail with an equal amount of stuffing. Combine the salt, garlic powder, black pepper, cayenne, and paprika, and lightly roll each quail in the seasoning mixture. Drape a bacon strip around each quail, place quail in a roasting pan, and roast in the preheated oven for 12 minutes.

Pass the quail under a preheated broiler until lightly browned. Quail are done when the juices run clear after a toothpick is inserted into a thigh. Do not overcook.

Spoon a portion of the heated Port sauce on each of four serving plates, and place two quail on top of each. Serve immediately.

Makes 4 servings

SAUSAGE SWEET POTATO BAKE

Julie Frankenfield of Godshall's prepares this simple, delicious dish for her husband, Steve, who said that they eat a lot of it during the winter months. Try substituting wine, beer, or turkey stock for water.

1 pound sage turkey sausage, casing removed

2 medium sweet potatoes, peeled and thinly sliced

3 medium Granny Smith apples, peeled and thinly sliced

Topping:

1 tablespoon sugar

1 tablespoon flour

$1/4$ teaspoon ground cinnamon

$1/4$ teaspoon salt

$1/2$ cup water

Preheat oven to 375° F. In a medium skillet, brown the sausage, breaking up larger pieces. Drain excess fat from the pan. Layer the sliced sweet potatoes, then the sliced apples, and top with the browned sausage in a greased 2-quart casserole.

Combine the topping ingredients and pour over the other ingredients in the casserole. Cover and bake for 50 to 60 minutes, or until the sweet potatoes are done.

Makes 4 servings

TURKEY LONDON BROIL WITH BEER AND HONEY

Butterflied turkey breast, which Godshall's markets as "turkey London broil," is an easy, tasty, and healthful dish, said Julie Frankenfield. But remember that when using a marinade for a sauce, bring the juices to a boil in a separate saucepan and simmer for 5 minutes to kill any bacteria that may have accumulated.

1 cup honey

2 tablespoons chopped fresh sage or 1 tablespoon dried

2 teaspoons chili powder

1½ teaspoons dry mustard

2 tablespoons fresh lemon juice

Salt to taste

3 cups beer

1 turkey London broil, 2 to 2½ pounds

In a bowl, combine honey, sage, chili powder, dry mustard, lemon juice, and salt. Slowly pour in the beer, and whisk until all ingredients are well combined.

Place the meat in a shallow pan, and pour the marinade on top. Refrigerate for 6 to 8 hours, turning several times to coat evenly with the marinade.

To cook, remove turkey from the pan and reserve the marinade. Place the turkey on a broiler pan and broil about 4 inches from the heat source for 15 to 20 minutes, or until cooked through, turning several times during cooking and basting with reserved marinade.

To serve, cut the turkey in thin slices against the grain. Pour any remaining marinade into a saucepan, bring to a boil, simmer for about 5 minutes, and serve with turkey.

Makes 4 servings

CHICKEN CASSEROLE

Eva Godshall takes this casserole to many of her church functions and suggests always cooking extra chicken for use in this recipe.

Oil or butter, for greasing	1 teaspoon salt
4 slices white bread, cubed	$\frac{1}{4}$ teaspoon pepper
2 cups diced cooked chicken	2 eggs, beaten
2 tablespoons chopped fresh parsley	$1\frac{1}{2}$ cups chicken broth
	$1\frac{1}{2}$ cups milk

Preheat oven to 350° F. Grease a large casserole dish with the oil or butter. Place a layer of bread cubes on the bottom of the dish, and add a layer of chicken, parsley, salt, and pepper. Continue in alternate layers, ending with bread cubes.

In a bowl, beat the eggs, add the broth and milk, pour mixture over the chicken, and bake for 45 minutes. Serve immediately.

Makes 6 servings

Market Customer: Eileen Etchells

Native-born Philadelphian Eileen Etchells, who has lived in Philadephia for many years, walks from her 6th Street townhouse to Reading Terminal Market to shop at least two or three times a week. Despite the changes she has seen over the years, she says she is glad that the market has not only survived but has retained its farmers' market image. Her visits always include a stop at Godshall's Poultry because, she said, "all their poultry is organically reared." Here is one of her recipes, a great entertaining dish that uses boneless chicken breasts.

CHEESE-STUFFED CHICKEN BREASTS

$3/4$ cup cream cheese

$1/3$ cup blue cheese

5 tablespoons butter

Pinch of grated nutmeg

$3/4$ cup grated Swiss cheese

4 chicken breasts, skinned and boned

2 tablespoons Dijon mustard

1 egg, beaten

$1/3$ cup flour

$1/4$ cup stale bread crumbs

$1/4$ cup olive oil

Bring the cream cheese, blue cheese, and butter to room temperature, place in a bowl, and cream together until smooth. Add nutmeg to taste and form into 6 ovals. Place the grated Swiss cheese on a plate and roll each oval in the cheese. Chill for at least 1 hour.

Flatten the breasts slightly between sheets of wax paper. Spread the breasts with the Dijon mustard. Place a cheese oval in the center of each breast and enclose it completely with the chicken.

Have ready 3 separate bowls containing the egg, flour, and bread crumbs. Roll each chicken breast in the flour, then in the beaten egg, and finally in the bread crumbs. Chill the chicken on a plate for about 1 hour.

Preheat oven to 400° F. In a heavy, ovenproof skillet, heat the olive oil and sear the chicken breasts for 2 to 3 minutes, or until they are lightly browned. Transfer the pan to the oven and bake for about 7 minutes.

Makes 4 servings

Harry G. Ochs Meats

Four generations of the same family make the Harry Ochs meat business one of the oldest continually run food purveyors in the nation. The business was started in 1906 by the grandfather and father of the present owner, Harry Ochs III.

A reputation for selling only the finest meats and Harry III's gregarious personality make the stand a centerpiece of the market – as does the massive black-and-white photo that graces the outer wall of the Ochs walk-in refrigerator. The photo, taken in Reading Terminal Market, shows Harry III as a child, his father, a case filled with meats, and price cards that read 47 cents for smoked tongue, 87 cents for smoked butt, and scrapple for 20 cents a pound; those cards guarantee that no passer-by will mistake this for one of the new market stands.

"My father worked here 66 years, I've worked here 48 years, and now my son is with me. I still have the straw hats my father wore at the shop – Stetsons. They are old now, but I wouldn't part with them for anything. I also sport a hat, not a straw one, but a cap." His sons won't wear hats.

Many prominent people have visited the market, either to shop or to simply browse, but, Ochs said, "My greatest thrill to this day was when I prepared cuts

Harry Ochs, Sr. and his son display their wares.

of meat for Joe DiMaggio and for Julia Child when she was in town for a cooking-show tour."

Ochs is a past president of the Reading Terminal Market Merchants Association and was a highly visible figure during the market's trying months of renovation. Many a time he was called upon to maintain the market's standards while city officials on one side and fellow merchants on the other fumed.

Ochs related story after story about the market while he deftly demonstrated his technique of boning a leg of lamb. Customers leaning up against his butcher block have watched him cut, trim, and prepare meats for years, while he shares recipes, ideas, tips, and local news. The whole routine has gone on for as long as anyone can remember. The tradition is carried on by his son, who is teaching his own 14-year-old the art of butchering.

They are one of the few butcher shops in the city that still carry hanging aged beef instead of boxed or Cryovac meats, which Harry IV said have less flavor. "We all have our special jobs. Mine is to prepare the crown roasts, while Dad does most of the boning and rolling. We all pitched in one Christmas season to prepare 400 fillet roasts."

Harry Ochs IV works side by side with his father and is delighted at the prospect of keeping his family's meat dynasty intact. "I can't think of anything I'd rather do than keep this stand going for a few more decades," he said.

BRAISED VEAL SHANKS

Harry Ochs III has many tips and recipes he shares with his customers. This veal dish is one of many he recommended we try for this book. The center of the shank bone has a fatty substance, marrow, that the osso buco connoisseur considers a real treat. Remove the cooked marrow by scooping it out with a special marrow fork or with a small demitasse spoon.

6 to 8 veal shanks, each approximately 2 inches thick

Olive oil, for coating veal and vegetables

3 cloves garlic, finely chopped

$^1/_2$ cup chopped Italian (flat-leaf) parsley

1 tablespoon chopped fresh rosemary or $^1/_2$ teaspoon dried

4 carrots, diced

1 large onion, chopped

2 medium potatoes, quartered

Salt and freshly ground pepper to taste

2 cups white wine

Preheat oven to 350° F. Generously coat veal shanks with olive oil. In a Dutch oven, brown the shanks on both sides over medium heat for about 5 minutes per side. Add garlic, parsley, and rosemary, and cook for 1 to 2 minutes. Coat carrots, onion, and potatoes with a little more olive oil, and add them to the Dutch oven. Season with salt and pepper, cook 2 to 3 minutes, and add the wine.

Bake, covered, in the oven for approximately $1^1/_2$ hours, or until veal is very tender and almost falling off the bone. If the wine evaporates too quickly during cooking, add more as necessary until shanks are cooked. Uncover and cook 15 to 20 minutes longer to reduce sauce and brown shanks lightly.

Makes 4 servings

ROAST BONED LEG OF LAMB WITH ROSEMARY AND WHITE WINE

This lamb dish reflects the elder Harry Ochs' Italian heritage from his mother, especially the use of the fresh herbs that are found in many Italian dishes. The flavors permeate the lamb and result in a juicy, succulent roast.

$\frac{1}{4}$ cup olive oil

1 cup dry white wine

4 cloves garlic, smashed

$\frac{1}{2}$ cup chopped Italian (flat-leaf) parsley

2 tablespoons chopped fresh rosemary

2 whole sprigs of rosemary

1 teaspoon freshly ground pepper

1 leg of lamb, boned and rolled, about $4\frac{1}{2}$ to 5 pounds

Make the marinade by combining the olive oil, wine, garlic, parsley, rosemary, and pepper. Place the lamb in a plastic bag and pour in the marinade. Seal bag, place in a shallow pan, and refrigerate for 6 to 8 hours, turning the bag over once or twice.

About 30 minutes before cooking, remove lamb from refrigerator and bring to room temperature. Preheat oven to 350° F.

Remove lamb and rosemary sprigs from marinade, and place meat in a roasting pan. Pour some of the marinade over the lamb. Cook, uncovered, for approximately $1\frac{1}{2}$ hours for rare, or 2 hours for medium, basting occasionally with reserved marinade. A thermometer inserted into the center of the lamb should register 140° F. for rare, 160° for medium. During cooking, add water to the pan as needed to prevent drippings from drying out.

Remove from oven, place lamb on a platter, and allow to sit for 5 to 10 minutes before slicing. Bring pan juices to a boil along with any juices that may have accumulated on the platter, and serve with the lamb.

Makes 6 to 8 servings

Market customer: Ronnie Colcher

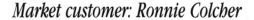

O ne of the most loyal customers of Harry G. Ochs Meats is Ronnie Colcher of Center City Philadelphia, the director of the HIV/AIDS Addiction Program at Valley Forge Medical Center & Hospital. She has been a market patron for more than 20 years.

"I only buy from Harry," she said. "Even in the summer, I take his meats to Maine. He packs them to travel, tells me cooking times and temperatures. He takes care of me and my guests."

She has been cooking since she was a little girl, and one of her favorite recipes is made with one of the Ochses' favorite products.

BARBECUED VEAL STEW

Colcher created this dish by also using ingredients from other merchants. The tangy barbecue sauce is from Moyer's, the salsa from 12th Street Cantina. A tip for removing excess fat: The stew can be chilled overnight, causing the fat to rise to the top, where it can be removed with a slotted spoon. Then simply reheat. Like most stews, making this one ahead improves the taste.

4 pounds well-trimmed veal breast, cut into 2-inch cubes

Flour, for dredging

2 tablespoons butter

2 tablespoons vegetable oil

$^1/_2$ cup tangy barbecue sauce

$^1/_2$ cup mild salsa

$^1/_2$ cup water

$^1/_2$ cup ketchup

2 tablespoons dark brown sugar

2 tablespoons Dijon mustard

1 tablespoon Worcestershire sauce

1 cup chopped celery

1 large Bermuda onion, thinly sliced

Preheat oven to 325° F. Dredge the veal cubes in the flour. Place the butter and oil in a large skillet, and brown the veal on all sides. Drain meat, remove from skillet, and place in a casserole. Combine the barbecue sauce, salsa, water, ketchup, sugar, mustard, and Worcestershire. Add the sauce to the casserole, and add the celery and onion to the dish. Bring to a simmer on the stovetop.

Transfer casserole to the preheated oven, and cook for 2 hours, making sure that the mixture is at no more than a simmer. If liquid evaporates during cooking, add a little water. If sauce seems too thin, uncover for the last 20 minutes of cooking time.

Makes 6 servings

Spataro's

"Drink Buttermilk and Live Forever."

This is a merchant who believes in his product. As the sign makes clear, Spataro's trademark is buttermilk. In the 1930s, Spataro's used to bring in old-fashioned buttermilk direct from the farmers and would churn out its own. People would pass by on the 12th Street side of the market and watch through the windows. Today, the Spataros – Domenic Spataro Sr. and Domenic Jr. – are not permitted to do it that way. Instead, they buy their cultured buttermilk in bulk from a dairy. It comes in 6-gallon containers, which they siphon off with a hose. Spataro's sells about 18 gallons of buttermilk a week, but as Domenic Sr. said, "In the old days we sold about eight times that amount."

Today's customers not only buy a glass of buttermilk to drink with their sandwich, but some of Spataro's Polish customers buy buttermilk to use in some of their potato dishes. Domenic Spataro Sr. started his career in the market during the 1930s by working after school at the Troelsch deli stand owned by the Stevens family. This stand was the forerunner of today's heath-food shops and sold whole-wheat muffins and raw vegetable sandwiches. In 1947, the Stevens family sold the business to Domenic Spataro and his wife, Dorothy. "I remember vividly, as it was just two weeks before Thanksgiving," he said.

Customers enjoy lunch at one of three Paulson's Buttermilk Counters, which stood in the market from the early 1930s until the late 1950s.

Domenic and his son Dom shared reminiscences. Domenic Sr. remembered the horses and carts, which were used for pickups and deliveries around the city. And he recalled the 1940s, when Philadelphians holding ration coupons waited in long lines to buy milk and butter at what was practically the only place in the city selling these items. Hanging dressed poultry, some with feathers still on, and sides of meat swinging from hooks were all around the market.

As the two Spataros chatted, wearing cheerful smiles on their faces and working side by side slicing meat and making sandwiches for customers, they recalled the days when a live train station operated above the market and when commuters would stop by first thing in the morning for coffee and order their meat from Harry Ochs. They'd return to Spataro's at lunchtime for a sandwich – with buttermilk, of course. And then, on their way home, they'd come by again to pick up their meat from Harry.

"You saw these regulars two or three times a day, each day, you got to know them. Life is different now," said Domenic Sr. "There is no train station above, and today, the young people are not too fond of buttermilk. They like meat and poultry cut up, ready to go."

Sandwiches then cost only 10 cents each (13 cents for ham and cheese, one of Spataro's most popular). Root beer – from the barrel – was a favorite beverage, too.

Frank Popow, former owner of another market favorite, Stella's, joined the conversation. When Popow sold, his good friend Domenic, whom he'd known since they were kids, offered Frank a job, so Frank decided to continue working at the market. He remembers when some scenes of the movie *Blow Out* were filmed in the market. In the background was Stella's, he recalled, and he made sure that everyone on his staff was in the picture. He mentioned that Rudy Valley and Preston Foster would visit the market, too.

Spataro's Cream Cheese and Olive Sandwich

When asked which is their most popular sandwich, Dom Jr. and Sr. both said the cream cheese and olive sandwich, which they have been making since Domenic Jr. took over. This wonderful, moist sandwich is a popular lunchtime item at Spataro's. All the Spataro's sandwiches are filled with quality ingredients and are large, tasty, and well-priced.

2 slices rye or whole-wheat bread

2 ounces cream cheese

2 tablespoons chopped green
olives with pimentos

2 lettuce leaves

2 or 3 tomato slices

Spread both pieces of bread with cream cheese. Top one slice with olives, lettuce, and tomato. Top with second slice of bread. Cut in half and serve.

Makes 1 sandwich

BUTTERMILK WHEAT BREAD

Dom Spataro's recipe for buttermilk wheat bread is delicious. (More so, perhaps, because he always drinks a bottle of beer when he makes it.) Spataro's creamy buttermilk gives the bread a nice, moist texture. Buttermilk originally was made from the residue left over from buttermaking, with butter granules added. Today, buttermilk is produced from pasteurized skim milk and a culture is added to develop flavor and consistency. Buttermilk is lower in fat and more easily digested than whole milk.

Butter or oil, for greasing pan	$\frac{1}{2}$ cup sugar
$2\frac{1}{2}$ cups buttermilk	1 extra-large egg
$2\frac{1}{2}$ teaspoons baking soda	$1\frac{1}{2}$ cups all-purpose flour
4 tablespoons ($\frac{1}{2}$ stick) butter, softened	$2\frac{1}{4}$ cups whole-wheat flour

Preheat oven to 350° F. Use the butter or oil to grease two 8 x 3 $\frac{3}{4}$ x 2 $\frac{3}{8}$ loaf pans. In a bowl, mix the buttermilk and the baking soda until the soda has dissolved. Set aside. In another bowl, cream butter and sugar, stir in the egg, and mix well. Add the buttermilk mixture to the creamed sugar, gradually stir both flours into the batter, and mix until ingredients are just blended but not smooth.

Divide between the prepared pans, and bake for approximately 1 hour. The bread is done when a toothpick inserted in the center comes out dry. Remove bread from oven and let cool for 5 to 10 minutes. Turn loaves out of pan, and cool completely.

Makes 2 loaves

L.D. Bassett Inc.

Ice cream was not invented in Philadelphia, but Philadelphia is nonetheless considered the ice-cream capital of the world. So what do most out-of-town-ers want to sample when they visit Philadelphia? And what do Philadelphians need to fulfill a craving for a sweet? A scoop of hand-dipped ice cream from Bassett's.

"Not only have generations of families enjoyed our ice cream at the market, but they have also taken many a pint home," said Michael Bassett Strange. One of the most popular Bassett's flavors has always been – and still is – vanilla.

Bassett's began in 1861, when Louis Dubois Bassett, a Quaker schoolteacher, began making ice cream in the back yard of his Salem, New Jersey, home, in a churn that was turned by a mule. He sold his ice cream, along with home-grown produce, from a stand on Market Street in Philadelphia. In 1893, along with many other merchants, Bassett moved to the newly built Reading Terminal Market.

Louis Lafayette Bassett, perfecting the recipe handed down from his grand-father, would comb the fruit and spice stands to find ingredients for exotic, new flavors, such as guava, kiwi, papaya, yellow tomato, and even borsht sherbet, which was specially prepared for a visit by then Soviet Premier Nikita Khruschchev.

Over the years, the reins and secret recipes were handed down, and Bassett's is now in the hands of Ann Bassett, the great-granddaughter, and Michael Bassett Strange, the great-great-grandson of Louis Dubois. Bassett's, like others among Reading Terminal Market's original "families," has survived the Civil War and the Great Depression. It has thrived now through five generations.

MRS. B'S APPLE CRISP

Grandmother's apple crisp is one of the Bassett family's favorite desserts. Their popular vanilla ice cream goes very well with this pie.

Butter, for greasing

5 large, tart apples (such as Granny Smith or Rome), peeled, cored, and sliced

$1/2$ cup water

1 teaspoon ground cinnamon

$3/4$ cup all-purpose flour

3 tablespoons butter

1 cup brown sugar

Vanilla ice cream

Preheat oven to 350° F. Place apple slices in a buttered, 9-inch-square baking dish. In a bowl, combine the water and cinnamon, and pour over the apples. Place the flour in another bowl, and add the butter and brown sugar. Work the mixture into coarse crumbs, and sprinkle the crumb mixture over the apples.

Bake for approximately 1 hour, or until lightly golden. Serve warm or at room temperature with ice cream.

Makes 6 servings

Eugene M. Moyer & Son

Scrapple conjures up different images to different people (the less familiar it is, the less favorable that image is likely to be), but many who taste it for the first time become avid scrapple lovers. Scrapple ingredients have changed from area to area as scrapple became more popular, but Christian F. Moyer developed his own recipe for scrapple in 1856, and it has not changed to this day. Meanwhile, scrapple has become a Philadelphia favorite.

It's the cornmeal that makes scrapple unique. A popular yarn regarding an old Philadelphia family describes the visit of Edward VII, then the Prince of Wales, to Philadelphia. Upon his return to England, he was said to speak of a breakfast he had eaten and reported that he had "a remarkable dish called Biddle and met a family named Scrapple." Not quite, but the Biddle family and the scrapple meal have both thrived.

The Moyer family came to Reading Terminal Market in 1904. Bob Moyer said that the company was started in 1856, "as close as I can figure," when Christian F. Moyer, his great-great-grandfather, went door to door in the city with a horse and wagon selling pork products in winter, corn and tomatoes in summer, and scrapple in September. The butcher shop at their homestead in Blooming Glen, Bucks County, still functions.

Bob Moyer remembers his parents bringing him and his sister to the market and placing them in a basket on the floor while they continued working. "We grew up in the market," he said.

To his eye, the most striking change over the years has been the eating habits of customers. Gone are the traditional roasts. Instead, his customers want quick and easy foods. He has adapted to these changes and sells a variety of cuts that lend themselves to easy grilling and pan-frying or microwaving.

Moyer is well known for his award-winning hams, which have a light, smoky flavor.

SCRAPPLE

Traditionally a breakfast food, scrapple is typically served with eggs and warm maple syrup. Most people are generally misinformed about scrapple. It has less fat than many think and, because of the cornmeal and buckwheat flour with which it's made, it is very nutritious. Perfectly cooked scrapple needs some time. The idea is to get a nice, crisp crust on the top and bottom while keeping the center soft.

1 meaty pork neck bone, cut into 2-inch pieces

1½ pounds pork cubes from shoulder

½ pound pork trimmings

½ pound pork liver

Water

½ cup cornmeal

Salt and freshly ground pepper to taste

¾ cup buckwheat flour

Vegetable oil, for frying

Place pork neck bone, pork cubes, trimmings, and liver into a large saucepan and cover with approximately 6 cups of water. Bring to a boil, reduce heat, and simmer for 1½ to 2 hours. When meat is very tender, remove from broth, strain the broth, and pour 3½ cups of it back into the saucepan. Reserve, and discard remaining broth.

Remove meat from neck bones. In the bowl of a food processor fitted with the steel blade, combine all the meats, and process until coarsely ground.

Over low heat, gradually pour the cornmeal into the reserved broth, stirring constantly until smooth, approximately 10 minutes. Add the ground meat to the cooked cornmeal, and stir to mix. Season with salt and pepper.

Add the buckwheat flour to the mixture, and cook for about 10 minutes, or until thickened. Pour mixture into loaf pan, let cool for 30 minutes, and refrigerate for 24 hours.

Remove from refrigerator, and cut into ⅜-inch slices. In a large skillet, heat oil until hot, and pan-fry scrapple, in batches, over medium heat for about 10 minutes on one side until nicely browned and crisp, then turn and cook about 5 minutes on the other side. Serve.

Makes 6 to 8 servings

HAM SPREAD

The Moyers don't waste a thing. This recipe was developed by experimenting with leftover ends of smoked hams. Now it is a popular item and wonderful for sandwiches or party spreads.

1 pound smoked ham

2 hard-cooked eggs

$^1/_2$ cup sweet gherkins, with juice

1 tablespoon prepared mustard

$^1/_3$ cup pitted black olives

$^3/_4$ cup sandwich spread

Place ham into a food processor or blender, and mix until just ground. Add remaining ingredients, and blend well. Serve with crackers or use as a sandwich filling.

Makes 3 cups

SMOKED SAUSAGE STEW

Lorraine Moyer suggests using their smoked sausage in this easy, tasty dish. In the spring when fresh peas are readily available, use instead of frozen peas and add a little mint to the dish.

1 pound smoked sausage

1 14½-ounce can crushed tomatoes

1 12½-ounce can French onion soup

2 medium potatoes, peeled and cubed

1 teaspoon Worcestershire sauce

1 package (10 ounces) frozen peas or ½ pound fresh peas, shelled

2 carrots, peeled and diced

Cut the sausage into ¼-inch slices and brown on all sides in a medium skillet. Drain off the fat, and add the crushed tomatoes, onion soup, potatoes, Worcestershire sauce, and fresh peas, if that's what you're using, and carrots. Bring to a boil, reduce heat, cover, and simmer for about 20 minutes, or until vegetables are tender. If you're using frozen peas, add them to the sausage 10 minutes after the simmering begins, and continue cooking until the potatoes are tender.

Makes 4 servings

CHAPTER 2   *The Lunch Counters*

Reading Terminal Market awakens at 8 a.m. and by the noon lunch hour, people from all walks of life are making their way to their favorite food stalls or venturing to try a new food experience. As we make our way down the aisles of eateries, we are struck by the sights, sounds, and aromas of the market – all of which illustrate how the market is as great a place to sit down and eat a meal as it is to find ingredients to take home and make a meal.

One might want to start with breakfast at Reading Terminal Market's only diner, the Down Home Diner. Jack McDavid, one of Philadelphia's most famous restaurateurs and a man whose name has become synonymous with "down-home cooking," can be found wandering around, wearing his coveralls and his trademark "Save the Farm" cap, greeting people in his measured Southern accent. McDavid is committed to maintaining the ambiance of a diner as an attraction to the market. Breakfast is popular here, with huge portions of cheese grits or red-eye gravy with biscuits and ham that bring back memories of hearty, old-fashioned breakfasts. From mid-morning on, the line for seating includes a mix of students, lawyers, bankers, judges, and office workers – all waiting patiently for a table to enjoy the hospitality and comfort foods that McDavid offers. Some of the lunch and dinner choices are good reflections of the ambiance: Breaded Catfish, Potlikker Stew with Country Ham and Turnip Greens, Po' Boy Catfish Sandwich, or Pulled Pork Barbecue with Butter Beans.

Right next door is By George Pasta and Pizza, where owner George Mickel is busy baking fragrant and flavorful pizzas, stromboli, and calzoni in the brick oven. As you walk past, glance at cases filled with fresh and frozen ravioli, tortellini, gnocchi, and homemade sauces – many of them choices for a meal ready to take home. Take a minute to watch fresh pasta dough being cut into different widths and to look at the many prepared Italian specialties – from lasagnas to simmering trays of juicy sausage, pepper, and onion. A panorama of multicolored peppers, sun-dried tomatoes, mounds of marinated fresh mozzarella, and hot peppers filled with provolone complete the picture.

Salumeria Italian Specialties, a colorful and well-stocked stand that conveys the essence of the market, will next catch your attention. If it's lunchtime, the line will tell you that it has caught a lot of other people's attention, too. Ed Sciamanna has captured the Italian flavor of his offerings with his displays of prosciuttos, salamis, and garlic dangling from the ceiling as well as his abundance of domestic and international cheeses. In one corner, large earthenware jars are filled with green and black olives, such as Gaeta and Calamata. Here you can find familiar ingredients as well as harder-to-find ones, such as mortadella and pancetta. At the takeout counter, people welcome the robust hot dishes and wait patiently in what can become an extremely long line. Some of the choices are unusual, such as a unique version of the standard hoagie (marinated artichoke hearts are one of the optional additions that can make Salumeria's Italian hoagies different from the many others available at the market and in the city). The stand also features its house vinaigrette, made with balsamic vinegar.

Across from Salumeria, you may notice some patrons peering at tanks filled with lobsters and Dungeness crabs. The Coastal Cave Trading Company Inc., owned by Steven Cho, has become Reading Terminal Market's specialist for shellfish, smoked fish, and caviar. From Maine, where the fish is cured over fruitwood for a mild and delicate flavor, to Scotland's and Norway's smoked salmon, many different varieties are available for sampling. For lunch, splurge on a whole Maine lobster, or fill your plate with crabcakes or lobster burgers. From Coastal Cave's raw bar, try oysters and clams shucked for you while you wait.

Then there's America's favorite sausage – the hot dog. At Franks A-Lot, owner Russell Black has been well recognized for his success with that humble food. His secret is to serve lean and tasty sausages with no added fats or fillers and with nicely seasoned meats that are stuffed into natural casings. These sausages can be seen slowly broiling on a roller grill until they are lightly golden. Unusual toppings accompany these traditional franks. The pizza-and-hoagie dog and the traditional Texas Tommy and chili dog have been acclaimed by many lunch customers as the market's best. Black has also perfected the french fry. His are popular and different, a cross between a potato chip and a regular french fry. We caught Pat Moyer of Eugene M. Moyer & Son, sitting at the counter enjoying a plateful of these addictive fries. "The best in town," she said.

Adjoining Franks A-Lot is the Tokyo Sushi Bar. This is one of many market establishments that showcase the tradition of immigrants opening restaurants, and it provides a wonderful opportunity for exploring many different food cultures. Sitting there puts you face to face with an attractive display of sushi, sashimi, and lightly coated tempura. You will often see owner David Dinh expertly preparing these famous Japanese dishes while pots of noodles, wontons, dumplings, and soups are gently simmering in the background. His seaweed and miso soup is excellent on a cold day.

Aroma alone makes you aware of some market stands, such as the aroma of freshly roasting turkey at Bassett's Original Turkey. Roger Bassett started this business by offering just one sandwich – turkey, lettuce, and tomato. It became so popular that he branched out and created a whole turkey theme. Now he offers fresh, hand-carved turkey, turkey platters, pot pies, and homemade soups. "All we do is turkey," said Roger Bassett as we watched thick slices of the juicy meat being served on freshly baked, cut-to-order breads.

When you approach the Basic 4 Vegetarian Snack Bar in the middle of the market, notice the pots bubbling with delicious vegetable stews. Pies and quiches are piled on the counter, their fillings varying according to the creative ideas of owner Alfoncie Austin. Austin's vision when she creates her vegetarian offerings is guided by the elements of a balanced daily diet – the four basic food groups: proteins, grains, fruits, and dairy products.

As you walk along the center court, you spot Jill's Vorspeise. "Vorspeise" is a German word that Jill Horn remembers her grandmother using frequently. The word refers to "things eaten before the main meal." Her business has developed from hors d'oeuvres to healthy foods. Popular lunch items include her vegetable pizza and her "veggie wedgie," both made with her own bread, and an ample array of grain, bean, and pasta dishes. Horn often has something new, exciting, and tasty to try, and a color-coded menu board helps customers make selections to suit their dietary needs. This is truly food for thought.

The Wok Shop is just a step away. Pea Fun Wang (better known as Anna) and Lie Wa Chang are originally from Taiwan, and their food reflects their heritage. Everything is cooked to order, and you can watch noodles and rice being tossed in large woks along with vegetables, chicken, or beef.

Anna's son Brian Wang and his wife, Jennifer, returned from Taiwan in 1987 and opened the Four Seasons Juice Bar, which is adjacent to the Wok Shop. Their freshly blended natural juices range from carrot, celery, and beet to kiwi, pineapple, and banana. Year round, customers are refreshed by these healthy juices, all of which are made without sugar, preservatives, or additives.

Just around the corner is Delilah's, one of the market's African-American-owned businesses. Delilah Winder, the vivacious owner, has brought her expertise – Southern cooking – to the market. Word of mouth sends customers flocking to her restaurant, where they sit and enjoy her modified soul-food dishes (modified by sharply cutting down on the fat). Some of the traditional Southern favorites she pointed out were fried chicken, barbecued ribs, cornbread, and black-eyed peas. Delilah has catered a reception for the opening of Duke Ellington's jazz opera "Queenie Pie" and was also involved in catering for members of Congress attending the "We the People 200" celebration in 1987.

Across the same aisle is Makis Fireworks, an eatery well described by a sign that says, "Come to know the thrill of the grill." That's a reference to owners Kelly and Makis Syrros's unusual sandwich combinations. Here are the sounds of sizzling hamburgers, soft-shell crabs (in season), and chicken or lamb with brie – all being grilled to perfection and smelling wonderfully of outdoor cooking.

Respect for good food is an integral part of the Chinese way of life. There are five main regional styles of cooking in China, and The Golden Bowl brings to the market the flavors and tastes of the Szechuan region. Pan Kai Maw and husband Michael Maw opened their stand in 1983, and their son David does most of the preparation and cooking of their dishes. He also prides himself on his sauces, some of which he makes with bean paste, hot chili peppers, or surprising additions of Worcestershire.

Polina Lender, originally from Russia, is the delightful owner of Salads Unlimited. She has created a cross-culture of European dishes ranging from quiches and an Athenian pasta to herrings in cream or wine sauce, bagels with lox and cream cheese, knishes, and homemade desserts. We watched as she poured batter into pans for a German cake ready to be baked for the next day's customers.

Close by is Kamal's Middle Eastern Specialties. Kamal Albarouki and his wife, Rose, arrived in the United States in the mid-'70s and ran a small grocery in South Philadelphia. In 1983, they opened a business in the market. You'll often see the Albaroukis' two young sons helping out behind the counter while Kamal and Rose are busily preparing a myriad of Middle Eastern favorites, including falafel and their popular Moroccan chicken.

What may be Philadelphia's best-known culinary invention – the cheesesteak – is well represented in the market by a third generation of the original Pat's King of Steaks. Until late in 1995, the stand was known by its familiar South Philly name, but Rick Olivieri changed the name to Rick's Philly Steaks when he bought the stand from his father. Cheese became part of the sandwich in the 1940s and the same Olivieri innovation is served today at Rick's Steaks. Like his grandfather, Rick Olivieri has a talent for invention. His Philadelphia Steak 'n Eggs breakfast is a must to try.

Another well-known stand is Rocco's Famous Italian Hoagies. Rocco DiGuglielmo has won Best of Philly awards in 1994 and 1995 for his stand's authentic Italian hoagies, prepared with imported lunch meats, roasted peppers, and real aged provolone cheese – premium ingredients that make a delicious sandwich.

The Greeks consider hospitality an essential part of their life, even more so when it includes food. We found George Voulgaridis and his son, Athens, the enthusiastic owners of the Olympic Gyro, glad to discuss their foods with us. We sat and watched a beef gyro turning on a spit and happy customers munching chicken and lamb souvlaki, all served on pita covered with tzaziki, a cucumber and onion topping.

Relax at the white-tiled counter and sitting area of the 12th Street Cantina, where colorful piñatas hang decoratively above, and you will enjoy a whole line of contemporary and traditional Mexican dishes. Owner Michelle Leff is considered the market's aficionada on all things Mexican. Michelle's travels in Mexico led her to explore local cuisines and to perfect tortilla recipes. At first, she made tortillas right at her stand. Now the tortillas are made locally, using her recipe. Her repertoire of Mexican foods has earned her a good reputation, and she has worked hard to find the ingredients that make her foods authentic. You will find the display cases and shelves filled with fresh and dried chilies, cactus plants, many different salsas, jars of mole, beans, and fresh tortillas. Every day, Michelle and her staff prepare many different dishes that you can sample for lunch or take home for a wonderful taste of Mexico at dinnertime. It's a cuisine that has been far more successful at this stand in the market than it has been at most other Mexican restaurants in Philadelphia.

Salad Express, owned by Ray DiSimone Food Group, is managed by John Iovine. Each day, a different selection of hot and cold buffet-style foods, as well as a special of the day, is served. Betty Thompson, the chef, creates many of these recipes, from Chinese noodles and rosemary chicken to traditional meat loaf and macaroni with beef. A salad bar of impeccably fresh ingredients is featured daily.

In the streets of Hong Kong, many food stalls have tempting arrays of mahogany-colored duck and other meats hanging in the doorways and windows. A stroll past Sang Kee Peking Duck shows how owner Michael Chow has captured that atmosphere with a rich display of hanging ducks and beef ribs. His menu board offers many different suggestions for serving duck – with rice, with noodles, and in soups.

Dinic's is a popular sandwich stand that is run by a father-and-daughter team. "Dad loves to cook," says Marcella Nicolosi, owner Tommy Nicolosi's daughter. Each day, they both arrive early to supervise the cooking of their specialties – pork, beef, and veal roasts. Slow oven roasting produces meats that are succulent and juicy. Many market merchants choose Dinic's as a place to relax and savor a hearty sandwich.

Right across is Sandwich Stand. Owner Bill Dellaratta runs this luncheonette, where stacks of lunch meats, cheeses, and home-baked breads are piled on the counter, together with different garnishes to choose from. One of his specials was created by two local television personalities, Joe Lerario and Ed Feldman, who host a program on PBS called "Furniture on the Mend." The sandwiches are called "Furniture Guy Joe's" (turkey and roast beef) and "Furniture Guy Ed's" (corned beef, American cheese, and raw onion). Dellaratta enjoys creating unusual sandwiches and interesting names for them, like the St. George Special (so called because it's supposedly hearty enough to give its eaters the energy to slay dragons), which he said was a favorite of Philadelphia Mayor Ed Rendell.

The Beer Garden operates amid a constant hustle and bustle of people, and it fills up quickly at lunchtime, so get there early if you want a table where you can enjoy your lunch and sip on beer or wine. This well-established place, owned by Tony Novelli, is a great meeting spot. It serves draft beers, imported and domestic bottled beers, and more specialized brands such as Samuel Adams and Dock Street, as well as Guinness stout, Bass ale, and various wines and sodas.

Down Home Diner's Cheese Grits

Grits are a staple in the American South – and at Down Home Diner. Hominy grits are ground hulled corn, white in color and mild in flavor. When cooked, the dish has a thickish texture.

1 cup quick grits

$2^1/_2$ cups shredded Cheddar cheese

$1/_4$ pound (1 stick) butter, softened

$1/_2$ cup milk

Generous dash of hot pepper sauce

Pinch of garlic salt

2 eggs, beaten

Preheat oven to 350° F. Grease a 2-quart casserole. Cook the grits according to package directions, place the cooked grits into a large saucepan, and add $1^1/_2$ cups of the cheese, the butter, milk, hot pepper sauce, and garlic salt. Cook over low heat until cheese has melted, remove from heat, and stir in the beaten eggs.

Pour the mixture into the casserole dish, sprinkle the remaining cheese on top, and bake for 45 to 60 minutes, or until set.

Makes 6 servings

MEAT LOAF

Dark soy sauce is a good ingredient to have in your cupboard. It is a dark, rich, and robust sauce, used mainly for gravies and marinades. Only a little is needed because of its strength. Betty Johnson uses it when she makes the gravies for some of her dishes at Salad Express.

2 pounds ground beef	1 large egg, beaten
1 green pepper, grated	4 cups water
2 cloves garlic, minced	2 beef bouillon cubes
1 medium onion, finely chopped	$1/4$ teaspoon freshly grated black pepper
2 tablespoons steak sauce	
1 tablespoon chopped parsley	1 tablespoon cornstarch
$1/4$ cup bread crumbs	1 tablespoon dark soy

Preheat oven to 350° F. Grease a standard loaf pan. In a large bowl, thoroughly mix the beef, green pepper, garlic, onion, steak sauce, parsley, bread crumbs, and beaten egg, place in the prepared loaf pan, and bake in a preheated oven for 1 hour.

To make the gravy, place the water, bouillon cubes, and pepper into a saucepan, bring to a boil, reduce heat, and cook until the cubes have dissolved. Sift in the cornstarch, and cook until thickened, about 3 to 4 minutes. Add the soy sauce, stir well, and serve over the meat loaf.

Makes 6 to 8 servings

TURKEY NOODLE SOUP

When Bassett's Original Turkey makes this soup, it's made in large quantity, and the soupmakers have an advantage over the home cook: a copious supply of juices and fat from all the roasted turkeys. This recipe, adjusted for home use, calls for turkey or chicken stock, but if you happen to have some juices from a recently roasted turkey, use them toward the 3 quarts of stock in the recipe.

3 quarts turkey or chicken stock

2 ribs celery, diced

1 large onion, diced

2 carrots, diced

1 cup chopped parsley

2 cups chopped tomatoes

1 tablespoon "crazy salt" (see note)

1 teaspoon basil

$^1/_2$ pound noodles

$^3/_4$ pound cooked turkey, cut into chunks

Place stock in a large saucepan. Add celery, onion, carrot, parsley, tomato, "crazy salt," and basil, bring to a light boil, reduce heat, and simmer for 1 hour. Add noodles and turkey chunks, stirring lightly. Let simmer for 15 minutes, stirring occasionally, until noodles are done and turkey is cooked through.

Note: "Crazy salt," used in this recipe, is a blend of salt, marjoram, and oregano. It's sold in many supermarkets, and, at Reading Terminal Market, premixed at Margerum's and the Spice Terminal.

Makes 8 servings

SUSHI

Sushi-making is an art in Japan, requiring many years of apprenticing before one is declared to have mastered it. Sushi means "vinegared rice," and, depending on local products, each region has its own specialty. Of the many varieties of seaweed, nori is the most common and is available in dark-green sheets. Wasabi is a very hot paste, similar to horseradish, made from the powdered root of the wasabi plant. You can buy it prepared, or you can mix a small amount of water with a little wasabi powder and stir until smooth. This recipe comes from David Dinh of The Sushi Bar.

$2^{1}/_{4}$ cups Japanese sushi rice, or short-grain white rice

$2^{1}/_{4}$ cups water

$^{1}/_{4}$ cup Japanese rice wine vinegar

6 sheets of nori (seaweed)

6 ounces smoked salmon or smoked bluefish, evenly sliced about 1/8-inch thick

Pickled ginger, for garnish

Wasabi (Japanese horseradish), for garnish

Rinse rice several times in plenty of cold water, drain, and set aside in a bowl for about 30 minutes.

Place rice in a heavy saucepan or steamer, and add the $2^{1}/_{4}$ cups of water. Bring just to a simmer, cover with a tight-fitting lid, and cook for about 20 to 25 minutes. If you're using a steamer, follow the manufacturer's instructions. When the rice is done, remove it from the heat, place it in a bowl, cover with a cloth or paper towel, and let it sit for 10 minutes.

Drizzle the rice wine vinegar over the rice, mix lightly with a fork, cover, and set aside to cool. The rice should be slightly warm so that the grains will stick together when rolling.

Place a bamboo sushi mat on a flat surface with the short edge nearest to you. Cover the mat with 1 sheet of nori, scoop 1 cup of the rice onto the nori, and pat the rice into an even layer all the way to the sides. (If rice sticks to your hands, dip your hands in water.) Leave a $^{1}/_{2}$-inch border at the top and bottom edge of rice. Place 1 slice of the smoked fish across the bottom of the rice.

Using both hands, fold the bottom edge of the nori around the filling to form a "log," at the same time pushing the mat away from you. End with the seam side underneath. Squeeze gently to smooth out the roll. Remove mat and repeat the procedure with the remaining ingredients. You'll become more proficient with each of the 6 rolls.

Dip a sharp knife into water, and even off the ends of each roll. Cut each roll crosswise into 8 even pieces, wiping and wetting the knife after each cut to help you cut cleanly.

Serve sushi pieces cut side up on a platter with some pickled ginger and wasabi on the side.

Makes 6 servings

Miso Bean Soup with Tofu and Seaweed

Miso is an inspired Japanese culinary invention made by boiling soybeans, mashing them, and adding rice, wheat, or barley in different proportions and then fermenting. Store unused tofu under refrigeration in plenty of cold water and change the water daily. The tofu and the miso are the basis for this soup, which is served at The Sushi Bar.

6 cups water	3 tablespoons white miso
1 sheet kambu seaweed, cut into strips	$\frac{1}{2}$ pound soft tofu, diced
	2 scallions, chopped, for garnish

Place the water in a large saucepan, and bring to a boil. Remove from heat, add the seaweed, and soak until softened. Remove the seaweed, reserving the water.

In a small bowl, make a paste by mixing the miso with 2 tablespoons of the reserved broth. Bring the reserved broth to a simmer and gradually stir in miso paste until dissolved. Add tofu and simmer gently for a few minutes, but do not bring to a boil.

Ladle into hot soup bowls and garnish with chopped scallions. Serve hot. If you wish, garnish the soup with some of the soaked seaweed, which will impart a slightly bitter flavor.

Makes 4 servings

867

SMOKED TROUT WITH ARUGULA, TOMATO, AND GOAT CHEESE

Arugula is a dark, leafy green with a distinct peppery flavor that complements the smokiness of the trout fillets. Most of the smoked fish served at the Philadelphia Lobster and Fish Company comes from Maine and is smoked in a combination of apple, red oak, black cherry, and sugar maple woods.

12 cloves unpeeled garlic

2 shallots, unpeeled

$\frac{1}{2}$ tablespoon sugar, or to taste

1 teaspoon salt

1 teaspoon black pepper

1 cup olive oil

4 smoked trout fillets, about 8 ounces each

1 bunch arugula, washed

2 to 3 ripe tomatoes, depending on size, sliced

1 "log" ($5\frac{1}{2}$ ounces) chèvre (goat cheese), cut in 4 slices

Preheat oven to 350° F. Place the garlic cloves and shallots on a baking tray, and roast for about 15 to 20 minutes, until soft. Remove from oven, let cool, and peel.

Place the garlic, shallots, sugar, salt, and black pepper in a blender or food processor, and mix until garlic and shallots are coarsely chopped. With the machine running, gradually add the oil and continue processing until the mixture has a fairly smooth consistency.

Place 1 trout fillet on each plate, surround each with some of the arugula and tomato, and place a slice of goat cheese on top. Stir the dressing, and drizzle some over each serving.

Makes 4 servings

New American Lobster Grill

The staff at the Philadelphia Lobster and Fish Company is knowledgeable, energetic, and creative when it comes to discussing their selection of smoked fish, shellfish, and caviar. They will split the live lobster for you, but you should cook it as soon as possible.

4 live lobsters, each $1\frac{1}{4}$ to 2 pounds

Rub:

$\frac{3}{4}$ cup olive oil

$\frac{1}{3}$ cup fresh lime juice

$2\frac{1}{2}$ tablespoons garlic, mashed

$\frac{1}{2}$ cup finely chopped cilantro

Freshly ground black pepper

Pinch salt

Prepare grill or barbecue. Split the lobsters through head and almost through tail, enough to open wide. Combine the oil, lime juice, garlic, cilantro, pepper, and salt. Wash out the chest cavities and crack the claws. Rub the marinade over the lobsters, and let sit for 10 minutes.

Drain excess marinade from the lobsters and place them on the grill, shell side down, for about 3 to 5 minutes. Turn them over, and cook for 2 minutes more, or until done.

Note: The lobsters can be served with lemon wedges, clarified butter, salsa, or caper mayonnaise.

Makes 4 servings

SMOKED FISH SPREAD

Vary the fish in this recipe according to availability and your own preference. The recipe comes from Philadelphia Lobster and Fish Company.

8 ounces cream cheese, softened

$1/4$ cup sour cream

3 tablespoons white horseradish

1 tablespoon lemon juice

$1/2$ pound smoked fish, skin removed, broken into chunks

Assorted vegetables or black bread

In a food processor or blender, combine the cream cheese, sour cream, horseradish, and lemon juice until smooth. Add the fish and process just until blended. Place mixture in a bowl and serve with vegetables or black bread.

Makes about 2 cups

GUACAMOLE

This is a popular dish and a favorite of the 12th Street Cantina. If you prefer a creamier version, prepare in a food processor or blender by processing all the ingredients together until smooth. Prepare this shortly before serving to prevent the avocado from discoloring. To help ripen avocados quickly, place them in a brown paper bag, and let sit at room temperature for a few days.

4 medium-sized ripe avocados, peeled and sliced

1 tomato, diced

1/4 cup finely chopped onion

1 clove garlic, minced

1/2 teaspoon paprika

Juice of 1 lime

1 to 2 jalapeño peppers, seeded and chopped

Salt and freshly ground black pepper to taste

In a large bowl, mash the avocado with a fork. Add the remaining ingredients and combine thoroughly. This produces a slightly chunky version.

Makes about 2 cups

MICHELLE'S SHRIMP ENCHILADAS

Michelle Leff, owner of the 12th Street Cantina, offers her primer on ingredients frequently found in Mexican dishes: Poblano chilies are dark green and about 5 inches long, tapering down to a point. They are medium hot and have a wonderful smoky flavor when roasted. Serrano chilies are bright green or red, about 2 inches long, and are hot but not bitter, great for making salsas. Tomatillos are yellowish-green with papery husks that should be removed before using. When raw, they are quite tart, but they have a more lemony flavor when cooked. And here's a tip for taking the heat out of chilies: Slice them lengthwise, and remove the rib and seeds.

12 poblano chilies

3 tablespoons olive oil

5 cloves garlic, minced

1 small onion, diced

2 pounds medium shrimp, shelled and deveined

6 ears corn, removed from the cob, or 5 cups canned corn

$1/2$ teaspoon Mexican oregano

5 sprigs fresh cilantro, chopped

2 fresh serrano chilies

Salt and freshly ground pepper to taste

Green enchilada sauce:

10 tomatillos, husks removed

4 cloves garlic, minced

2 serrano chilies

1 medium onion, chopped

Salt and freshly ground black pepper to taste

2 teaspoons Mexican oregano

2 tablespoons vegetable oil

10 sprigs fresh cilantro, chopped

Pinch sugar

Additional vegetable oil, for dipping

12 fresh corn tortillas

2 cups sour cream or crème fraîche

Roast the poblano chilies over an open flame, or broil them until charred. Place in a plastic or paper bag for about 10 minutes. Remove from the bag, peel the skin from each chili, and cut into strips. Reserve.

In a skillet, heat the oil and sauté garlic and onion for 1 to 2 minutes. Add the shrimp, corn, and half of the poblano chilies, and cook another 2 to 3 minutes. Add oregano and cilantro, remove from heat, add the serrano chilies, and season the mixture with salt and pepper. Reserve.

To make the green enchilada sauce, bring a large saucepan of water to a boil, blanch the tomatillos for 15 minutes, and drain. Place the tomatillos in a blender or food processor with the garlic, remaining poblano chilies, the serrano chilies, onion, salt, pepper, and Mexican oregano, and blend until smooth.

In a small saucepan, heat the 2 tablespoons of vegetable oil, add the tomatillo mixture, reduce heat, and simmer for about 20 minutes. Add cilantro and sugar. Remove from heat and reserve.

To prepare the enchiladas, preheat oven to 325° F. Heat about 1 inch of oil in a medium skillet. Holding the fresh tortillas with tongs, dip quickly into the hot oil for about 5 to 10 seconds. Drain on paper towels.

Dip each tortilla into the reserved tomatillo sauce, and place a portion of the shrimp mixture on one side of each tortilla. Fold each tortilla in half. Place them on two baking sheets. Cover the sheets with foil, place in oven, and heat through for approximately 10 minutes.

Remove and serve topped with sour cream or crème fraîche.

Makes 12 servings

FILET OF BEEF YUCATAN

The tortillas sold at the 12th Street Cantina are made with stone-ground white corn, not from a mix. The consistency is more traditional, a little thicker and tastier than the commercial ones.

1 bulb garlic

4 cloves

1 teaspoon dried thyme

3 allspice berries

$\frac{1}{2}$ teaspoon black peppercorns

$\frac{1}{2}$ teaspoon cumin seeds

1 tablespoon cider vinegar

1 teaspoon honey

$\frac{1}{2}$ teaspoon salt

4 steak filets, each about 5 ounces

2 tablespoons corn oil

12 (1 package) 6-inch corn tortillas, warmed

Preheat oven to 325° F. Place the garlic bulb in a small baking dish, and roast until softened, about 30 to 40 minutes.

Meanwhile, in a dry skillet, lightly toast the cloves, thyme, allspice berries, black peppercorns, and cumin seeds. Toss the spices a few times to brown them evenly, about 5 minutes. Be careful not to burn the spices.

Finely grind the spices and place them in a small bowl. Squeeze the cloves of the roasted garlic from their skins and place the garlic cloves with the spices. With a fork, mash into a paste. Add the vinegar, honey, and salt. Marinate the steaks in this paste for 3 to 6 hours. Brush the steaks with corn oil, and grill to desired doneness. Slice and wrap in warm tortillas.

Makes 4 servings

STUFFED GRAPE LEAVES

The following recipe is a favorite among Kamal Albarouki's customers at Kamal's Middle Eastern Specialties, which sells the ingredients for many Middle Eastern dishes.

1 16-ounce jar grape leaves

2 large onions, finely chopped

2 bunches Italian (flat-leaf) parsley, minced

$1/4$ cup fresh mint leaves, chopped

$1\frac{1}{2}$ cups short-grain rice, rinsed

3 tomatoes, peeled, seeded, and finely diced

1 cup olive oil

1 teaspoon salt

$1/4$ teaspoon allspice

$1/4$ teaspoon nutmeg

Juice of $1\frac{1}{2}$ lemons

2 potatoes, peeled and sliced, any variety

1 lemon, cut into wedges, for garnish

Cover the grape leaves in cold water and soak for 15 to 20 minutes. Rinse, drain, and pat dry. Trim the stems off the leaves, and reserve 8 or 9 large leaves.

In a bowl, combine onion, parsley, mint, and rice. Add tomato, oil, salt, allspice, nutmeg, and juice of 1 lemon, and combine thoroughly.

Place 1 grape leaf with its dull side up on a work surface, and place a heaping teaspoon of the filling near the stem end. Fold in the sides and roll up the leaf. Repeat with remaining leaves.

Line the bottom of a deep saucepan or roasting pan with the sliced potatoes, and top with the reserved large grape leaves. (This protects the filled grape leaves from sticking.) Place the rolled leaves in layers, close together and seam side down. Put a dinner plate on top to keep rolls in shape during cooking. Mix the remaining lemon juice with enough water to barely cover the grape leaves. Cover with a lid, bring to a boil, reduce heat, and simmer for approximately 45 to 60 minutes, or until the rice in the filling is cooked. (Break into one to test the rice.) Add more water during cooking if the water in the pot evaporates too quickly.

Cool, remove grape leaves from saucepan, and serve garnished with lemon wedges.

Makes 10 to 12 servings

MOROCCAN CHICKEN

The spice mixture in this recipe from Kamal's is made in a quantity far larger than what you'll need. The unused portion freezes well and can be used in other recipes. A lot of liquid will remain after roasting; reserve that liquid and use it as a base for soups or for cooking rice.

2 bunches Italian (flat-leaf) parsley

1 medium onion, quartered

$1/4$ cup garlic powder

2 tablespoons ground coriander

2 tablespoons ground ginger

1 tablespoon black pepper

Salt to taste

2 chickens, each 3 to $3^1/_2$ pounds

Fresh coriander, for garnish

In a food processor or blender, process the parsley and onion, add garlic powder, ground coriander, ground ginger, black pepper, and salt, and blend to a smooth paste.

Preheat oven to 350° F. Spread $1/_2$ cup of the spice mixture on the bottom of a baking dish. Place the chickens on top and add enough water to cover the chickens. Bake, uncovered, for approximately $1^1/_2$ hours, or until chicken is very tender. Cut chicken into serving pieces, and place on a platter with some of the pan juices. Garnish with fresh coriander.

Makes 6 servings

STUFFED SQUASH

The use of cinnamon, fresh mint, and pine nuts is traditional in many Lebanese dishes. Kamal Albarouki of Kamal's Middle Eastern Specialties suggests using this stuffing for other vegetables such as peppers or eggplants.

1 pound ground lamb or beef

2 tablespoons pine nuts, toasted

1 large onion, finely chopped

$1/_2$ teaspoon ground cinnamon

2 tablespoons olive oil

$2^1/_2$ pounds ripe tomatoes, chopped

2 cloves garlic, minced

2 tablespoons chopped fresh mint

Salt and freshly ground pepper to taste

6 small zucchini, halved lengthwise, flesh scooped out

Preheat oven to 350° F. In a bowl, combine meat, pine nuts, onion, and cinnamon. Heat the oil in a medium skillet over medium heat, add the meat mixture, and sauté for about 10 minutes or until meat is well browned and the onion has softened.

In a large bowl, combine the chopped tomatoes with their juices, the garlic, mint, salt, and pepper.

Place the zucchini halves side by side in a large baking dish, and stuff each piece with a portion of the meat mixture. Press down gently to even the filling, pour the tomato mixture over and around the zucchini, and bake in the oven for about 25 to 30 minutes, or until zucchini are tender.

Makes 6 servings

Humus

Tahini, a paste made from sesame seeds, has a strong, nutty flavor. Lemon salt, another ingredient used here, can be purchased from Kamal's Middle Eastern Specialties and is used in many Middle Eastern recipes. You can make your own by combining 1 tablespoon of sea salt and the zest of 1 lemon.

2 cups canned chickpeas, rinsed and drained

3 cloves garlic, smashed

$1/2$ cup tahini

1 teaspoon lemon salt, or to taste

$1/2$ to 1 cup water

Pita bread, cut into wedges

Place the chickpeas and garlic in the workbowl of a food processor and blend. Add the tahini and lemon salt, and process until just blended. With the machine running, gradually add water until the mixture is smooth and creamy. Chill for several hours, bring to room temperature, and serve with pita wedges.

Makes about 2 cups

Cheese Lasagna

Preparing lasagna can be time-consuming, but using fresh pasta sheets eliminates a time-consuming step. The fresh pasta dough is available from By George Pasta and Pizza, the source of this recipe.

1 tablespoon chopped fresh parsley

1 clove garlic, minced

1 cup freshly grated Parmesan cheese

8 ounces mozzarella cheese, grated

6 cups tomato sauce

1 pound ricotta cheese

6 sheets fresh pasta

Preheat oven to 450° F. In a bowl, combine the parsley, garlic, Parmesan, and mozzarella.

Spread a little tomato sauce on the bottom of a 9 x 13 x 2-inch lasagna pan. Cover with a single layer of pasta, which will probably use exactly two sheets of pasta. Spread a thin layer of tomato sauce and ricotta cheese over the pasta. Sprinkle with one-third of the Parmesan mixture, and cover with another layer of pasta. Top with half the remaining tomato sauce, all the remaining ricotta, and half the remaining Parmesan mixture. Cover with a third layer of pasta. Top with remaining tomato sauce and remaining Parmesan mixture. Cover with foil, bake for about 20 minutes, remove foil, and bake for another 8 to 10 minutes, until cheese is bubbly. Let sit for about 5 minutes before cutting and serving.

Makes 6 servings

PEPPERONI STROMBOLI

Buy prepared bread dough for this dish, which is then assembled and ready for cooking in a short time. George Mickel of By George says to vary the filling according to your tastes and preferences.

$1^1/_2$ pounds bread dough	Oil, for greasing baking sheet
8 ounces shredded mozzarella cheese	1 small egg, beaten
$^1/_4$ pound pepperoni, thinly sliced	1 tablespoon sesame seeds

Preheat oven to 450° F. Cut dough in half, and stretch one piece into a round that is 9 inches in diameter. Place half the shredded mozzarella down the center of the dough, and top with half the pepperoni slices. Fold one side over the filling, overlap with the other side, tuck in the ends, and, using your fingers, pinch all the seams securely to seal. Repeat with the other piece of dough and the remaining mozzarella and pepperoni. Place seam side down on a greased baking sheet, brush with beaten egg, and sprinkle with sesame seeds.

Bake for 15 to 20 minutes, or until golden brown. Remove from oven, let cool for 5 minutes, and cut into 1-inch-thick slices to serve.

Makes 12 to 14 servings

TRI-COLOR TORTELLINI SALAD WITH ROASTED PEPPERS

This recipe from By George makes generous use of an Italian favorite, roasted peppers. A quick way to roast your own peppers is to preheat the oven to 425° F., slice the peppers in half, place on a baking sheet, and bake for 15 to 20 minutes, or until peppers are blistered. Let cool, and peel.

1 pound tri-color tortellini with cheese

4 roasted red peppers

Florets from 1 bunch broccoli

1 rib celery, chopped

1 carrot, sliced

2 tablespoons red wine vinegar

6 tablespoons olive oil

Pinch of oregano

Salt and freshly ground pepper to taste

2 tablespoons grated Parmesan cheese

1 tablespoon chopped parsley

1 clove garlic, minced

Place tortellini in boiling water and cook for about 7 to 8 minutes. Drain, run under cold water until cooled, and place in a large salad bowl. Prepare roasted peppers (see head note) and set aside.

Blanch the broccoli and carrots separately for 1 to 2 minutes in a large saucepan of boiling water. Run under cold water to stop the cooking. Add the vegetables in with the pasta.

Make the vinaigrette by whisking together the vinegar, oil, oregano, salt, and pepper.

Add the Parmesan cheese, parsley, and garlic to the pasta. Pour in the vinaigrette, and toss to mix thoroughly.

Makes 4 servings

MARINATED VEGETABLES

This recipe is one of Salumeria's most popular daily lunch specials. It's easy to make, and varying the vegetables seasonally will keep you from tiring of it. It makes a colorful addition to a buffet table.

Dressing:

$\frac{1}{2}$ cup chopped Italian (flat-leaf) parsley

1 cup extra-virgin olive oil

$\frac{1}{4}$ cup lemon juice

1 teaspoon salt

1 teaspoon pepper

3 medium cloves garlic, minced

Vegetables:

1 small zucchini, cut lengthwise and sliced into $\frac{1}{4}$-inch-thick pieces

1 yellow squash, cut lengthwise and sliced into $\frac{1}{4}$-inch pieces

$\frac{1}{4}$ pound mushrooms, cleaned and sliced

1 red bell pepper, cut into strips

1 head Bibb lettuce

To make the dressing, combine the parsley, olive oil, lemon juice, salt, pepper, and garlic in a blender or food processor, or shake in a jar. Reserve.

Place the zucchini, yellow squash, mushrooms, and red pepper in a bowl and toss them with the dressing. Allow to marinate 1 to 2 hours. Place the lettuce on a platter or in a bowl. Using a slotted spoon, place the vegetables on top of the lettuce, and sprinkle with the reserved dressing.

Makes 4 servings

SPICY SHRIMP

Have plenty of bread ready to mop up the juices from this tasty, do-ahead appetizer from Salumeria. Cooked marinades tend to bring out a more subtle and less sharp flavor than most noncooked marinades.

1 pound medium shrimp

1 cup olive oil

2 cloves garlic, minced

1 teaspoon freshly ground black pepper

1 teaspoon crushed red pepper flakes

$1/3$ cup hot pepper relish

$1/2$ cup lemon juice

Bring a large saucepan of water to a boil, add the shrimp, reduce heat to a simmer, and gently cook shrimp for about 2 minutes, or until they lose their raw look. Drain, cool, and peel the shrimp.

Make the marinade by placing the olive oil, garlic, pepper, pepper flakes, pepper relish, and lemon juice in a saucepan, and simmer for about 20 minutes. Let cool. Place marinade in a large bowl, add the peeled shrimp, and let marinate for 3 to 4 hours, or overnight.

To serve, remove shrimp from marinade with a slotted spoon, and pile into a large bowl.

Makes 4 to 6 servings

BROCCOLI AND MUSHROOM PASTA SALAD

Polina Lender of Salads Unlimited makes this delicious summer salad using all the fresh herbs that are available. The vinaigrette is characterized by the unusual addition of chopped tomatoes.

Tomato vinaigrette dressing:

1 medium onion, peeled and quartered

1 large tomato, quartered

3 tablespoons olive oil

3 tablespoons red wine vinegar

1 teaspoon dried mint or basil

$3/_4$ teaspoon salt

$1/_4$ teaspoon pepper

Salad:

3 tomatoes, coarsely chopped

$1/_2$ pound mushrooms, sliced

$1/_2$ pound corkscrew macaroni, cooked

2 bunches broccoli, broken into small florets and steamed

$1 1/_2$ cups croutons

To make the vinaigrette, place the onion, tomato, oil, vinegar, mint or basil, salt, and pepper in a food processor or blender. Cover and process until smooth. Toss dressing with chopped tomatoes and sliced mushrooms. Cover and refrigerate up to 24 hours. Just before serving, toss dressing mixture with hot cooked pasta and broccoli, and sprinkle with croutons.

Makes 6 servings

VEGETARIAN CHILI

This chili is an example of the healthful foods offered at Jill's Vorspeise. You have the option of using canned or dried beans. If you use dried, here's a quick way to soak them: Place the beans in a saucepan, cover with water, and bring to a boil. Remove the pan from the heat, and let the beans sit in the water for 1 hour. Drain and rinse thoroughly. Cook in water to cover for 1 hour or until soft, then proceed with the recipe. Wheat berries, lentils, and bulgur are quick-cooking grains that do not need any soaking.

1 tablespoon olive oil

2 cups diced onions

1 cup diced carrots

4 cloves garlic, finely chopped

1 tablespoon chili powder

2 teaspoons ground cumin

1 teaspoon ground coriander

1 teaspoon ground cinnamon

$1/4$ teaspoon cayenne

Freshly ground pepper to taste

1 28-ounce can Italian plum tomatoes

1 can water, from empty tomato can

$1/4$ cup wheat berries

$1/4$ cup lentils

2 15-ounce cans kidney beans, or 1/2 pound dried (see head note)

1 15-ounce can navy or great northern beans, or 1/4 pound dried (see head note)

1 15-ounce can black beans, or 1/4 pound dried (see head note)

$1/3$ cup bulgur wheat

In a large saucepan over low heat, heat oil and gently sauté the onions, carrots, and garlic about 10 minutes, or until softened. Add the chili powder, cumin, coriander, cinnamon, cayenne, and black pepper, and simmer for about 5 minutes, stirring frequently.

Add the tomatoes plus the can of water. Roughly break up the tomatoes with a wooden spoon, add the wheat berries, and simmer for $1/2$ hour. Add the lentils, and simmer another $1/2$ hour, or until lentils and wheat berries are tender. Add more water if liquid reduces too much. The mixture should be soupy rather than stewy. Add the cooked beans and the bulgur wheat. Stir gently over medium heat until bulgur has softened, about 5 to 6 minutes.

Makes 6 to 8 servings

SPANAKOPITA (SPINACH PIE)

Phyllo is a delicate, light, paper-thin, and flaky pastry. When working with phyllo, always cover the sheets with a slightly damp towel to keep them from drying out. You can substitute phyllo for the outer wrapper of any stuffed dish, such as wonton skins, eggrolls, tortillas, empanadas, or crêpes. Spanakopita is one of those classic Greek specialties that you never tire of, and this is an easy version from Olympic Gyro.

2 pounds fresh spinach, washed

4 large eggs, beaten

$^3/_4$ pound feta cheese, crumbled

Pinch of salt and pepper

12 sheets phyllo dough

Vegetable oil or melted butter, for brushing

Preheat oven to 350° F. Wash spinach thoroughly, place it in a large saucepan with the water still clinging to the leaves, and simmer gently until just wilted. Squeeze out as much water from the cooked spinach as possible, chop coarsely, and place in a bowl. Add beaten eggs, feta, salt, and pepper, and mix well.

Lightly brush a 14 x 18-inch tray with oil. Place 1 sheet of phyllo dough on the tray, and lightly brush it with the oil or melted butter. Repeat until you have used 6 of the phyllo sheets.

Spread the spinach mixture over the surface of the top sheet of dough. Then layer the remaining phyllo on top of the spinach mixture, again brushing each sheet with oil or melted butter. With a sharp knife, gently cut into squares, but do not cut all the way through. Bake for about 20 minutes, or until the phyllo is lightly browned.

Makes 6 to 8 servings

FRIED RICE

You can make this dish using leftover rice, shrimp, chicken, or pork. It's a dish that is a meal in itself, says Anna Wang, who owns The Wok Shop.

$\frac{1}{2}$ pound small shrimp

6 tablespoons vegetable oil

3 cups cooked long-grain rice

2 scallions, coarsely chopped

2 tablespoons soy sauce

Pinch sugar

1 cup bean sprouts

Shell the shrimp, slice them lengthwise in half, and cut each half into $\frac{1}{4}$-inch pieces. Heat a wok or large skillet over high heat, add 3 tablespoons of the vegetable oil, reduce heat to medium, add the shrimp, and stir-fry for 1 minute, or until shrimp are pink and firm. Set aside.

Wipe the wok with a paper towel, and reheat, adding the remaining 3 tablespoons of oil. Add the rice and scallions, and toss briskly. Pour in the soy sauce, add the sugar, and stir-fry, tossing quickly. Add the cooked shrimp, and stir-fry until all ingredients are heated through. Mix in the bean sprouts, and serve at once.

Makes 4 servings

SESAME NOODLES

Noodles symbolize longevity in China and come in various shapes and sizes, fresh or dry. American or Italian packaged noodles can be used as a substitute for the Chinese. All Chinese noodle dishes begin with boiled noodles, which are rinsed in cold water to remove the starch and are drained well before final cooking. Sang Kee Peking Duck prepares several noodle dishes, and this is one of them.

1 pound Chinese noodles, fresh or dried

1 12-ounce jar sesame paste

$\frac{1}{4}$ cup sesame oil

$\frac{1}{4}$ cup soy sauce

$\frac{1}{4}$ cup oyster sauce

$\frac{1}{4}$ cup red wine vinegar

Dash of chili oil

Pinch of sugar

1 cup shredded Chinese cabbage

1 cup shredded carrots

1 red pepper, thinly sliced

1 tablespoon rice wine vinegar

Bring a large saucepan of water to a boil, and cook the noodles. Drain and let cool.

In a bowl, combine the sesame paste, sesame oil, soy sauce, oyster sauce, red wine vinegar, chili oil, and sugar. Pour mixture over noodles and toss well. Place on a serving dish.

Combine the cabbage, carrots, and red pepper in a bowl. Mix in the rice wine vinegar, and toss well. Place the vegetables over the noodles, and serve at room temperature.

Makes 4 servings

Veal Scallopini

This mixture makes a juicy, finger-licking sandwich filling and is one of the many favorites served at Dinic's for lunchtime takeout. The filling is also good served over pasta or rice.

2 tablespoons olive oil

1 medium onion, chopped

3 cloves garlic, chopped

1½ to 2 pounds boned veal shoulder, cubed

1 cup red wine

1 to 2 sprigs fresh rosemary, or 1 teaspoon dried

2 tablespoons fresh parsley, chopped

¼ cup chopped fresh basil

1 teaspoon crushed pepper flakes

Pinch of salt

Freshly ground black pepper to taste

1 cup water

1 green pepper, sliced

2 cups crushed Italian tomatoes

8 Italian rolls, split, or 6 servings cooked rice or pasta

In a large saucepan over low heat, heat the oil. Add the onion and garlic, sauté for 2 to 3 minutes, add the veal cubes, and brown on all sides. Add the wine, rosemary, parsley, basil, pepper flakes, salt, and pepper, and simmer for 5 minutes. Add the water, and cook for another 4 to 5 minutes.

Add green pepper, and simmer until softened, about 5 minutes. Pour in the crushed tomato, and simmer gently for 40 to 50 minutes more, or until the veal is fork-tender. Add more water if too much liquid evaporates. The veal should be just covered lightly with the sauce. If using as a sandwich filling, spoon onto the split rolls. Or use as a topping for 6 servings of rice or pasta.

Makes 8 sandwiches or 6 topping portions

CHICKEN AND BRIE SANDWICH

This very tasty lunch sandwich is good enough to serve as a nice, easy dinner dish. The recipe comes from Makis Fireworks.

1 boneless and skinless chicken breast, split

2 tablespoons Dijon mustard

4 slices brie, each $\frac{1}{8}$-inch thick

4 slices bread, or 2 rolls of your choice

Grilled mushrooms and peppers (optional)

Brush chicken on both sides with mustard. Grill or broil chicken on both sides until cooked. Place a slice of brie over each chicken breast, run under a broiler until cheese has melted, grill or sauté mushrooms and peppers, if desired, and serve over the chicken or alongside each sandwich.

Makes 2 sandwiches

ST. GEORGE SPECIAL

Sandwich Stand's St. George Special is, according to Bill Dellaratta, a favorite of Philadelphia Mayor Ed Rendell.

1 tablespoon Russian dressing	4 thin slices pastrami
2 slices black bread	4 thin slices corned beef
4 thin slices roast beef	2 tablespoons coleslaw

Spread dressing on the two slices of bread. Place the meats on top of one slice, cover with the coleslaw, cover with the second slice of bread, press down lightly, and cut sandwich in half.

Makes 1 sandwich

DELILAH'S OLD-FASHIONED BANANA PUDDING

Delilah Winder grew up eating her godmother's variety of puddings. Chocolate Oreo is Delilah's favorite, strawberry is the favorite of Jackie Jones, her godmother, and this recipe for banana pudding is a favorite at her market stand, Delilah's.

2 tablespoons butter	2 teaspoons vanilla extract
$3/_4$ cup sugar	Zest of $1/_2$ lemon
3 eggs, lightly beaten	1 12-ounce box vanilla wafers
1 cup milk	6 ripe bananas, sliced
$1^1/_2$ teaspoons flour	6 egg whites

Preheat oven to 350° F. Make a sauce by placing the butter, $1/_2$ cup of the sugar, eggs, milk, flour, vanilla, and lemon zest in a medium saucepan over low heat. Cook until thickened.

Place a layer of wafers in a 9 x 13 x 2-inch baking dish, cover with sliced bananas, and pour the sauce over mixture.

In a bowl, beat egg whites until stiff, gradually add the remaining $1/_4$ cup sugar, and beat until you have a smooth meringue. Pour the meringue evenly over the banana mixture, and bake for approximately 20 to 25 minutes until the meringue is lightly browned. Serve hot or at room temperature.

Makes 4 to 6 servings

DELILAH'S SOUTHERN FRIED CHICKEN

This recipe appears to use a lot of hot pepper sauce, but the heat mellows considerably during the marinating process. The result adds just enough pep to this traditional Southern fried chicken. Delilah Winder is partial to Crystal hot sauce from Louisiana, and she makes a point of frying in canola oil.

1 6-ounce bottle of Crystal brand hot sauce

1 frying chicken, cut into pieces

Flour, for dredging

$\frac{1}{2}$ teaspoon salt

Canola oil, for frying

Place hot sauce in a large bowl, and marinate the chicken pieces in the sauce for several hours.

Combine flour and salt in a plastic bag. Place chicken parts in the bag, and shake well to coat with the mixture.

In a deep skillet, add enough oil to come three-quarters of the way up the sides. Fry the chicken, covered, for about 15 minutes, then uncover and continue frying for another 5 to 10 minutes, or until chicken is cooked through and nicely browned.

Makes 4 servings

RICK'S CHEESESTEAK

The secret of an authentic traditional Philadelphia cheesesteak, says Rick Olivieri, is no oil for the meat – just a spritz of water on the grill. Also, never chop the steak in pieces; just toss without breaking the meat so that it remains tender and moist.

1 tablespoon oil

1 small onion, thinly sliced

$\frac{1}{2}$ pound thinly sliced minute steak or chip steak

$\frac{1}{4}$ pound American, provolone, or mozzarella cheese (or the traditional topping—Cheez Whiz)

2 long Italian rolls, sliced

Place the oil in a small skillet, add the onion, and fry until golden. Heat a large skillet until hot, add the steak, moisten with a small amount of water, and quickly sear the meat on all sides. When the steak is almost ready, top with the cheese, allow to melt, and place on sliced rolls. Top with the onion, and serve.

Makes 2 sandwiches

CHILI DOGS

Their top-quality hot dogs and unusual toppings make Franks A-Lot different, says Russell Black, the stand's owner. The addition of beer and coffee gives a boost to this sauce.

1 tablespoon vegetable oil

1 large onion, sliced

1 green pepper, sliced

2 cloves garlic, minced

1 pound ground beef

Salt and freshly ground pepper to taste

$^3/_4$ cup draft beer

1 cup tomato sauce

1 to 2 tablespoons freshly brewed coffee

1 tablespoon chili powder

Place the oil in a medium skillet, and cook the onion, pepper, and garlic over low heat until softened, about 10 minutes. Add the ground beef and cook until well browned. Season with salt and pepper. Add the beer, tomato sauce, coffee, and chili powder, and cook about 20 to 30 minutes over medium heat, stirring often, until thickened. Serve in bowls as chili or as a topping for hot dogs on rolls.

Makes 4 servings of chili or enough to top about 12 hot dogs

Yu Shin Vegetable

David Maw was very emphatic about the use of some of the ingredients in this dish. He insists on using only Chinese cooking sherry, for example, and light soy sauce, which is less salty. He finds that dried garlic has a less garlicky flavor in this dish, but the use of Worcestershire sauce is the key.

Sauce:

1 cup chicken broth

1/2 cup dark sesame oil

1/4 cup Chinese cooking sherry

1 teaspoon freshly grated ginger

1 teaspoon dried garlic, or 2 cloves fresh chopped garlic

1 teaspoon Worcestershire sauce

2 tablespoons oyster sauce

1 teaspoon hot pepper oil

2 tablespoons sugar

1/4 cup light soy sauce

2 tablespoons vegetable oil

2 cloves fresh garlic, minced

Vegetables:

Florets from 1 bunch broccoli

2 carrots, thinly sliced

1/4 pound mushrooms, thinly sliced

1 rib celery, thinly sliced

1/2 cup sliced water chestnuts

6 to 8 dried Chinese mushrooms, softened in hot water for 10 minutes and drained

1 tablespoon cornstarch

In a bowl, combine the chicken broth, sesame oil, sherry, ginger, garlic, Worcestershire, half the oyster sauce, the hot pepper oil, sugar, and soy sauce, and set aside.

Heat a large skillet or wok, and pour in vegetable oil. Add garlic and the remaining oyster sauce, and mix well. Add broccoli, carrots, mushrooms, celery, water chestnuts, and Chinese mushrooms, and stir-fry for 2 to 3 minutes. Pour the sauce into the wok. When the sauce is boiling, sift in the cornstarch, and cook until slightly thickened. Serve with rice.

Makes 4 servings

ROCCO'S HEALTHY HOAGIE

Rocco's Famous Italian Hoagies created this "healthy hoagie" for hoagie-happy Philadelphia.

2 cups mixed uncooked vegetables (choose from zucchini, eggplant, mushrooms, broccoli rabe, hot pepper, sweet pepper, onion, fennel)

8 thin slices aged sharp provolone cheese

1 cup shredded romaine lettuce

2 plum tomatoes, sliced

2 10-inch-long Italian rolls

In a steamer, lightly steam the vegetables. On a hot grill or stovetop grill, quickly brown the vegetables for 2 to 3 minutes. Slice open each roll, and place half the lettuce, plum tomatoes, grilled vegetables, and cheese in each. Run under a broiler until the cheese has melted.

Makes 2 sandwiches

CHAPTER 3 .... *The Grocers*

Where else but in Reading Terminal Market do you get so strong a feeling for Philadelphia as a melting pot? The ethnic diversity of the groceries is reflected here, and you can take advantage of a great assemblage of international foods all available under one roof. Each grocery has its own personality and specialty.

The Giunta family has been in the meat business since 1912, first in Philadelphia's Italian Market, and since 1983, at Reading Terminal Market as Giunta's Prime Meats. In 1987, Martin Giunta took it over as a sausage store, along with a full line of meats and game, and the stand then took the name Martin's Quality Meats and Sausages.

As Martin Giunta's interest in sausage-making grew, he opened a sausage plant in South Philly, where he soon was producing many pounds and many varieties of sausages. Hot and mild Italian sausage, fresh apple sausage, Luganega sausage with Romano cheese and parsley, chicken apple sausage, fresh chorizo sausage – his list goes on and on. Martin Giunta's father, Charles, known as Mr. G. to his friends and customers in the market, is supposedly retired, but he's in every day, working behind the counter, making deliveries, or picking up meats.

In 1959, Siegfried Maldener brought his wife Marita, son Uwe, and daughter Elizabeth to settle in the United States from Saarbrucken in Germany. Maldener, who has been in the meat business all his life, soon moved to Philadelphia and opened a German delicatessen stall, Siegfried's and Son German Gourmet, in Reading Terminal Market. His meats, salamis, and sausages are all produced locally under his watchful eye in the traditional German way. Whenever Maldener's travels take him to Germany, he is on the lookout for different recipes and ideas to bring back and develop for the American market. Siegfried draws shoppers from miles around who come specifically to buy his authentic German specialties. These include homemade liverwurst and teawurst, both precooked, that can be used as patés or spreads. Homemade fresh sauerkraut, spatzle, herrings in wine, an enormous array of imported and domestic meats and sausages, together with German breads and mustard are sold at his stand, providing cooks with the ingredients for such traditional dishes as choucroute garni (see the recipe in this chapter).

Enjoy a sampling of tasty Thai food at the Thai Food Market, owned by restaurateurs Manoch and Somboon Pornmukda. The market sells deliciously prepared food for an eat-in lunch or a take-home dinner. Also available are many Thai ingredients, such as red curry sauce, fresh garanga, Thai hot pepper, sweet and spicy basil, ready-made Pad Thai sauce, and a variety of noodles, rice, and other grocery items.

Al Starzi, the owner of The Spice Terminal, established his spice connection in Philadelphia's Italian Market. But since 1981, he has been in business for himself in Reading Terminal Market. He is now helped by his nephew, Leonard Podagrosi, whose interest in retail started when he was a kid helping his uncle in the Italian market. Podagrosi manages this well-stocked place, which is filled to the brim with everything that the store's name would suggest – imported and domestic herbs and spices, jars of sauces, vinegars (including balsamic vinegars that range in price from $3.95 to $100 a bottle), and many olive oils – as well as many things that the store's name might not suggest, such as a full variety of coffee beans (a sight and aroma at the store's entrance), candies, and dried fruits.

The Reading Terminal Cheese Shop stocks imported and domestic cheeses. Owner Doug Johnson says that his customers' favorites include some exotic imports like Greek kasari, Canadian oka (a semi-firm Cheddar), a Dutch goat gouda called Benning, and a Norwegian cheese called Nokkellost with caraway and cumin. Johnson also sells many spreads that can be included in their special-order party trays.

The Pennsylvania General Store opened in the market in 1987. Michael and Julie Holahan conceived the store as a source for Pennsylvanian-made foods and crafts. They created a country-style general store whose shelves are filled with such familiar names as Wilbur chocolate buds, Great Valley Mills flours and mixes, and Asher's chocolate-covered pretzels and potato chips, which are piled high to tempt you as you walk by. Also displayed are many colorful Amish quilts. And here you can find Pennsylvania maple syrup, too. Gift baskets of Pennsylvania products are mailed nationwide, and the store's catalogue abounds with ideas.

Another part of the Holahans' business is The Reading Terminal Box Lunch, featuring sandwiches, salads, and freshly baked cookies and brownies, all prepared daily in their kitchen and all made using ingredients obtained in the market. Your lunch will arrive in an attractive box and can be delivered by staff members anywhere in the city.

When you are ready for an espresso, cappuccino, or caffé latte during a break or after lunch, Old City Coffee offers a great cup, and the aroma of freshly brewed beans is there for all passersby. Ruth Isaac Treatman owns this stand, which has been in the market since 1988 and is run by her husband, Jack, offering a remarkable selection of coffee beans from around the world, all carefully roasted on the premises. The choices are numerous, among them coffees from Guatemala, Brazil, Jamaica, and Kenya, along with a house blend that mixes Colombian, French, and Ethiopian beans. Beans are ground to order and are sold along with pastries and accessories for brewing and grinding your own coffee.

But you may prefer tea. Many people do. Hence, the Tea Leaf, an elegant tea shop owned by Lynnette Chen and offering an incredible range of teas from Europe and Asia. Chen's shop is the only one in the market devoted entirely to tea – black tea, green tea, oolong tea, flavored black teas, herbal teas, and decaffeinated teas.

Glen and Theresa Mueller have captured a child's – and adult's – dream of candy heaven with their old-time candy store, Chocolate by Mueller. Remember licorice twizzlers, candy cigars, hand-dipped chocolate marshmallow pops, and clear barley sugar toys? They're all there. More sophisticated offerings include exotic-looking chocolate-dipped grapes and strawberries, colorful marzipan, and rows and rows of gourmet chocolates and truffles.

MARITA'S CHOUCROUTE GARNI

At Siegfried's, you'll find a large selection of German sausages. This recipe, which goes well with hot German mustard, uses four kinds. Knockwurst is made with pork and beef. Bratwurst comes in three varieties (Hungarian, which is smoked; Beergarden, which is made from pork and veal; and Nurnberg, which is made with pork and veal and is seasoned with marjoram). Mettwurst is a smoked sausage. Wieners are made with beef and veal and are stuffed into natural casings.

$1/4$ pound bacon, diced

1 large onion, chopped

2 pounds fresh sauerkraut

$3^1/_2$ cups dry white wine

6 juniper berries, lightly crushed

2 bay leaves

1 Granny Smith apple, peeled, cored, and chopped

4 smoked pork chops

2 links bratwurst

2 links knockwurst

2 links smoked mettwurst

2 wieners (German frankfurters)

In a large saucepan or Dutch oven, cook the bacon until lightly crisp. Add onion and sauté until soft, about 5 minutes. Add sauerkraut, wine, juniper berries, bay leaves, and apple, and stir to combine. Bring mixture to a boil, reduce heat to a simmer, cover, and cook $1^1/_2$ hours.

Add smoked pork chops and all the sausage links, cover, and continue simmering for another 20 minutes.

Remove sausages and cut into approximately 2-inch lengths. Place sauerkraut on a large platter and top with the pork chops and the sausage pieces.

Makes 4 servings

STRAMMER MAX

This recipe's name refers to a strong and hearty sandwich. The name of the sandwich varies, depending on where in Germany it's found. Uwe Siegfried's favorite breakfast dish is this egg-and-ham sandwich from Saarbrucken, Germany. It has been a family favorite for many years. For an extra treat, serve it with a hollandaise sauce.

4 slices rye bread
4 eggs, cooked sunnyside up
4 slices Westphalian ham
4 slices Swiss cheese

1 tablespoon grated Parmesan cheese
Paprika, for garnish

Preheat oven to 350° F. Lightly toast bread. Place a cooked egg on each slice of toast, and top each with a slice of ham and a slice of Swiss cheese. Sprinkle each with a bit of Parmesan cheese, place on a baking sheet, and bake in the oven until the Swiss cheese just starts to melt. Sprinkle sandwiches with paprika and serve at once.

Makes 4 sandwiches

BAKED MONKFISH WITH HERBS

Pic-a-spice was created by Al Starzi of The Spice Terminal and is a mixture of garlic, onion powder, mustard, dill weed, chervil, and ground celery seed.

2 pounds monkfish	1 tablespoon pic-a-spice
1 tablespoon olive oil	3 lemon slices
Juice of $1/2$ lemon	1 cup white wine or clam juice

Preheat oven to 350° F. For each piece of fish, cut a piece of foil large enough to wrap around it. Place monkfish on the foil, drizzle with oil and lemon juice, sprinkle the spice mixture over the fish, and lay the lemon slices on top. Fold the foil securely around the fish and place on a baking tray.

Bake for 10 to 15 minutes, depending on the thickness of the fish. Remove from the oven, remove foil, and place fish on a broiling pan. Reserve any juices that collect in the foil. Heat the broiler and broil fish for about 4 to 5 minutes, until lightly browned.

While fish is broiling, pour reserved fish juices into a saucepan. Add the wine or clam juice, bring to a boil, reduce liquid slightly, and serve over fish, cut into serving pieces.

Makes 4 servings

PAD THAI

Pad Thai is a traditional Thai noodle dish. Manoch and Somboon Pornmukda, the owners of the Thai Food Market, carry many Thai ingredients, such as the dried noodles, tamarind (a sour-tasting fruit), preserved radish, fish sauce, and fried shallot used in this recipe.

1 pound rice noodles	1 tablespoon lime juice
3 tablespoons vegetable oil	1 tablespoon tamarind juice
20 small shrimp, peeled and deveined	1 tablespoon fried shallot
3 tablespoons diced tofu	3 tablespoons coarsely ground dry-roasted peanuts
1 tablespoon preserved radish	$1/8$ teaspoon ground chili, or to taste
3 eggs	
2 tablespoons sugar	2 cups bean sprouts
2 tablespoons fish sauce	2 garlic chives or scallions, sliced

Cover the rice noodles with warm water in a large bowl, and soak for 15 to 20 minutes, or until softened. Drain and set aside.

Heat the oil in a large frying pan or wok, add the shrimp, and sauté over medium heat until shrimp have turned lightly pink. Add the tofu and preserved radish, and cook for 1 minute more. Add the eggs to the pan and use a fork to break them up. Stir gently with the shrimp.

Add the noodles, sugar, fish sauce, lime juice, and tamarind juice, toss to mix, and cook over medium heat for about 5 minutes, until the noodles have softened. Add the fried shallot, peanuts, chili, half the bean sprouts, and half the garlic chives. Fold until ingredients are well mixed.

Remove from heat, and garnish with remaining bean sprouts and garlic chive.

Makes 4 servings

LEMONGRASS SHRIMP SOUP

The owners of the Thai Food Market, Manoch and Somboon Pornmukda, gave us this classic lemongrass soup recipe. Lime leaves have a unique, citrusy flavor and can be found at the Thai Food Market and other Asian markets. You could substitute a combination of grated lime zest and freshly squeezed lime juice to taste. This soup can also be made with two thinly sliced, boneless chicken breasts instead of the shrimp.

6 cups chicken stock

2 stalks lemongrass, sliced

4 lime leaves

1 tablespoon sweet or roasted chili paste

3 tablespoons fish sauce

$\frac{1}{2}$ pound small shrimp, peeled

Juice of 1 lime

Coriander leaves, for garnish

Bring the stock to a boil in a large saucepan over medium heat. Meanwhile, trim the lemongrass stalks, cutting away and discarding the grassy tops so as to leave the stalks about 6 inches long. Remove any hard root and discard the tough outer leaves. Slice the lemongrass into 2-inch pieces.

Stir the lemongrass, lime leaves, chili paste, and fish sauce into the broth, bring to a boil, and continue boiling for about 5 minutes. Add the shrimp, and cook for about 2 minutes. Add the lime juice, and pour into shallow bowls. Garnish with coriander leaves.

Makes 4 servings

Pasta with Meat Gravy

From Martin's Quality Meats and Sausages comes this recipe, the Giunta family pasta sauce. "We call it gravy," says Martin Giunta, following a South Philadelphia tradition.

Sauce:

$1/4$ cup olive oil

1 medium onion, finely chopped

3 cloves garlic, thinly sliced

4 basil leaves, coarsely chopped

2 28-ounce cans crushed tomatoes

1 can water (using tomato can)

Salt and freshly ground pepper to taste

Meats:

3 to 4 tablespoons olive oil

$1/2$ pound each lean shoulder cuts of beef, veal, and pork, cut into 2-inch cubes

2 cloves garlic, minced

Salt and freshly ground pepper to taste

$1/2$ pound Italian sausage (hot or mild), cut into 3-inch pieces

Meatballs:

$1/2$ pound each ground beef, veal, and pork

2 large eggs

$1/4$ cup grated Locatelli Romano cheese

1 cup bread crumbs (homemade are best)

2 tablespoons finely chopped Italian (flat-leaf) parsley

2 to 3 tablespoons olive oil

Pasta:

2 pounds spaghetti, fettucine, or penne

To make the sauce, heat the oil in a large saucepan over medium heat. Add onion, garlic, and basil, and cook until onion has softened, about 2 minutes. Add tomato, water, salt, and pepper, and simmer for approximately 10 minutes. Set aside.

To cook the meats, heat oil in a large skillet, and brown the beef, veal, and pork cubes in the hot oil, turning them often. Add the garlic, and season with salt and pepper. Add to sauce. Add sausage links to skillet and brown thoroughly. Add to sauce.

To make the meatballs, thoroughly combine all the meatball ingredients in a bowl. Form into balls, each about $1/2$ inches in diameter. Heat oil in a skillet and brown the meatballs. Add to sauce.

To finish the sauce, after the meats, sausage, and meatballs have been added, simmer the entire mixture for approximately $1/2$ hours. Cook your favorite pasta in a large pot containing at least 6 quarts of water, following package directions. Time the pasta to be finished at the same time as the sauce. Serve the sauce over the pasta.

Makes 8 to 10 servings

SAUSAGE SMOTHERED IN ONIONS AND TOMATOES

Martina Giunta offered us one of her sausage recipes, which makes generous use of the sausage made by Martin's Quality Meats and Sausages.

3 tablespoons olive oil

2 cups onion, thinly sliced

2 cups canned Italian plum tomatoes, chopped

Salt and freshly ground pepper to taste

1 pound sausage (any variety)

Place the oil and onion in a medium skillet, cover, and cook over low heat until the onion softens, about 5 minutes. Uncover and continue cooking over low heat, stirring occasionally, until onion has turned a deep golden color, about 15 minutes.

Add the tomato, salt, and pepper. Reduce heat, and simmer for about 20 minutes. With a fork, prick the sausage in several places and add whole to the tomato mixture. Cover the skillet and cook over medium heat for about 20 minutes, turning the sausage from time to time to cook evenly. Slice sausage and serve with sauce.

Makes 4 servings

BASMATI RICE WITH SAFFRON

Saffron is the world's most expensive spice. Dried crocus-flower stigmas are hand-picked, and each blossom yields only three stigmas to produce the saffron. It gives a beautiful yellow color and a subtle flavor to rice and other dishes. Buy it in threads, rather than ground, for fresher flavor. Before using saffron, always steep it in hot liquid to bring out its flavor. This recipe comes from an anonymous customer who frequently buys his spices and dried fruits at The Spice Terminal.

1 teaspoon saffron

3 tablespoons milk, warmed

2 cups Basmati or other long-grain white rice

2 tablespoons vegetable oil

3 cardamon pods

2 3-inch sticks cinnamon

4 cups water

$\frac{1}{4}$ teaspoon salt

In a small bowl, soak the saffron in the warmed milk for 10 to 15 minutes. Wash the rice well under cold water several times, until water is clear.

Heat oil in a medium-sized, heavy-bottomed saucepan. Place the cardamom and cinnamon sticks in the pan, and stir a few times. Add the rice and fry for 1 to 2 minutes, making sure that the rice is well coated with the oil.

Add the water and salt, bring to a boil, cover, reduce heat to a simmer, and cook for 15 minutes. Pour in the saffron liquid and toss lightly with a fork. Cover and cook another 10 minutes, or until rice is tender. Fluff the rice with a fork and serve.

Makes 6 servings

CHICKEN BRAISED IN VINEGAR

Katherine Podagrosi, whose son Leonard manages The Spice Terminal, has always cooked for a large family. Now, she says, there is only herself, her husband, and her son. This is one of Leonard's favorite dishes. Notice that it uses no oil or salt.

1 whole chicken, about 3½ pounds, cut into pieces and skinned

2 teaspoons ground rosemary

2 teaspoons garlic powder

1 teaspoon paprika

¼ teaspoon freshly ground black pepper

4 bay leaves

1½ cups red wine vinegar

Preheat oven to 350° F. Place chicken pieces in a baking dish, season with rosemary, garlic powder, paprika, and black pepper. Place bay leaves on top. Bake for about 10 minutes, or until the spices are nicely browned. Pour the vinegar on top, and cook for about 1 hour more, until the liquid has turned into a glaze. Remove bay leaves and serve.

Makes 4 servings

Market customers: Grant and Kathryn Greapentrog

G rant Greapentrog and Kathryn Keeler Greapentrog, longtime resi-
dents of Center City Philadelphia, are very active in the community and involved with institutions such as the Settlement Music
School. Both are interested in food and food events and have worked on
what may be the market's premier annual event, the "Valentine to the
Market." In addition, Kathryn is a member of the Reading Terminal Market
Trust Board. Every Saturday, they shop at the market, visiting many of the
merchants and getting an early start to beat the rush. Grant is the baker and
dessert-maker in the family, and this recipe is from the '50s, a dessert he
remembers being served during the holidays when he was a teenager. "It's
a kind of fruit cake for those people who say they don't like fruit cakes."

BRAZIL NUT LOAF

$1/2$ pound candied pineapple	$3/4$ cup sugar
1 cup maraschino cherries	$1/2$ teaspoon baking powder
1 pound pitted dates	$1/2$ teaspoon salt
1 pound whole Brazil nuts	2 large eggs
$3/4$ cup flour	1 teaspoon vanilla

Preheat oven to 300° F. Grease a loaf pan, and line it on the bottom
and sides with wax paper.

Cut pineapple into $1/2$-inch chunks, gently dry the cherries, and combine them in a large bowl with the dates and nuts. Combine flour,
sugar, baking powder, and salt. Sift the mixture over the fruits and
nuts, and mix until the fruits and nuts are well coated.

In a large bowl, beat the eggs until foamy and stir in the vanilla. Add
the fruits and nuts, and blend thoroughly.

Turn mixture into the prepared pan, spreading evenly, and bake on
the center shelf for $1^3/4$ hours, or until well set. Remove from oven
and let cool on a cake rack for 10 to 15 minutes. Remove from pan,
carefully remove wax paper, and allow to cool thoroughly on the
rack.

Wrap in foil and refrigerate. Slice when cold, then serve at room
temperature.

Makes 8 servings

MACARONI AND CHEESE

This creamy, classic macaroni and cheese recipe comes from the Reading Terminal Cheese Shop. Doug Johnson says the recipe's extra-sharp Cheddar cheese, which comes from Vermont, is one of his biggest sellers.

6 tablespoons butter
$\frac{1}{4}$ cup flour
$2\frac{1}{2}$ cups milk
Salt and freshly ground pepper to taste
$\frac{1}{2}$ teaspoon dry mustard

12 ounces grated extra-sharp Cheddar cheese
1 cup grated Parmesan
2 cups macaroni, cooked
$\frac{1}{2}$ cup fresh bread crumbs
Paprika

Preheat oven to 350° F. In a saucepan, melt 4 tablespoons of the butter over low heat, blend in the flour, and cook over low heat for 2 to 3 minutes. Remove from heat, add the milk, return to medium heat, and whisk until smooth. Season with salt, pepper, and mustard. Toss in all but 2 tablespoons of the Cheddar cheese, stir until melted, and remove from the heat.

Mix half of the Parmesan into the drained macaroni, then mix with the cheese sauce, and turn into a $1\frac{1}{2}$-quart, lightly greased casserole.

Bake, covered, in the preheated oven for 20 minutes, then increase the heat to 450° F. Sprinkle with the bread crumbs and the remaining Parmesan. Melt the remaining 2 tablespoons of the butter and drizzle on top, then sprinkle with paprika and remaining Cheddar cheese. Bake, uncovered, for 5 minutes more, or run under the broiler until golden on top.

Makes 4 servings

CHEESE FONDUE

This recipe from the Reading Terminal Cheese Shop reminds us of a popular Swiss tradition – that anyone who loses a piece of bread in the fondue must kiss the person sitting to the right.

1 baguette

1 clove garlic, halved

$1^1/_2$ cups dry white wine

1 tablespoon lemon juice

$1^1/_2$ pounds coarsely grated Swiss, Emmental, or Gruyère cheese, in any combination

Freshly grated pepper and nutmeg to taste

Cut the bread into thick slices, then into quarters, so that each piece has a crust on one side. Rub the interior of an earthenware fondue pot with the cut sides of a clove of garlic, set the vessel over medium heat, add the wine and lemon juice, and heat, but not to a boil.

Start adding cheese by the handful, stirring constantly in one direction with a wooden spoon. Each handful of cheese should melt and become thoroughly incorporated before adding the next. Make sure that the heat is distributed evenly to prevent the cheese from coagulating in the center. If this happens, it is better to start over rather than risk ruining all the cheese.When all the cheese has melted and the mixture has become smooth and creamy, season with pepper and nutmeg.

Keep the fondue warm over low heat as everyone dunks bread in the hot mixture and coats each piece with the bubbling cheese. If it gets too thick, add additional warm wine and stir until smooth.

Makes 6 to 8 servings

MOCHACCINO

This is a great 3 p.m. pick-me-up from Old City Coffee. To prepare this properly, you need a cappuccino maker equipped with a steam wand. The sweetness is adjustable and geared to an adult palate. To get a good foam, start with very cold milk and a pitcher that has been in the freezer for a few minutes. Steam, then allow to rest for a few minutes to help stiffen the foam. Old City Coffee makes this recipe with its six-bean espresso blend and brews it with a thick layer of "crema," which describes the top layer of foam, using freshly roasted and ground Arabica beans.

12 ounces whole milk

1 heaping tablespoon Dutch cocoa

Sugar to taste

4 ounces brewed espresso coffee

Whipped cream flavored with French vanilla syrup (optional)

Semisweet chocolate shavings (optional)

Steam milk in a steamer pot, and set aside. In a mug, combine cocoa and sugar. Add espresso and whisk quickly to dissolve cocoa. Pour the hot milk into the mug, and follow with the milk foam that remains. Top with whipped cream, and garnish with chocolate shavings, if desired.

Makes 1 serving

LYNNETTE'S PERFECT CUP OF TEA

Lynnette Chen uses one basic method of brewing tea, regardless of the variety. Black tea, such as Earl Grey, Lapsang Souchong, and Darjeeling, is made from tea leaves that are fermented, while green teas, such as Chinese Gunpowder, Japanese Genmaicha, and Sencha, are made from leaves that are steamed. Oolong tea, a common blend, is a combination of green and black tea leaves. There are also flavored black teas and herbal teas, which blend flowers, leaves, roots, seeds, fruits, and nuts, and are often brewed as health remedies.

To make a good cup of tea: Preheat the teapot by pouring boiling water into it, and let sit for about 5 minutes. Discard water and add tea. Use 1 teaspoon of tea leaves per cup. Pour boiling water over the leaves, and steep the tea. Green tea should steep for 3 minutes, black and herbal teas for 5.

MAPLE SYRUP QUICKBREAD

Maple syrup comes from the sap of the maple tree, and a good yield depends on the right combination of cool nights and warm days. At the beginning of spring, the syrup is quite clear, but it becomes darker and stronger-flavored as spring progresses. When the sap has been collected, it is boiled down, with 40 to 60 gallons of sap needed to produce a single gallon of syrup. Pennsylvania is the country's fourth largest syrup-producing state. This recipe, like the pure maple syrup it uses, comes from the Pennsylvania General Store.

$\frac{1}{4}$ pound (1 stick) unsalted butter, softened

1 tablespoon sugar

2 large eggs, beaten

$\frac{2}{3}$ cup buttermilk

$\frac{1}{3}$ cup maple syrup

1 cup whole-wheat flour

1 cup all-purpose flour

1 teaspoon baking powder

$\frac{1}{2}$ teaspoon baking soda

$\frac{1}{2}$ teaspoon salt

$1\frac{1}{2}$ cups coarsely grated apple (about 2 apples)

$\frac{1}{2}$ cup crushed walnuts

Cream cheese, for spreading

Preheat oven to 350° F. Grease a standard loaf pan and set aside. In a large bowl, cream together the butter and sugar, beat in the eggs, and pour in the buttermilk and the maple syrup. Stir just until mixed.

Into this mixture, sift the flours, baking powder, baking soda, and salt. Stir until well combined. Add the apple and walnuts, and mix gently.

Spoon batter into the prepared loaf pan. Bake for 50 to 60 minutes, or until a skewer inserted into the center comes out clean. Turn bread out onto a rack, and let cool completely. Slice and serve with the cream cheese.

Makes 1 loaf

APPLE BUTTER SPREAD

Traditionally, apple and other fruit butters were made in large copper kettles. The process took the whole day with everyone stirring until the fruit formed a butter-like consistency.

The Pennsylvania General Store carries a wide variety of fruit butters.

1 10-ounce jar apple butter   **6 ounces cream cheese, softened**

Place the apple butter and cream cheese in a food processor or blender, and process until smooth. Serve at room temperature on muffins, scones, cornbread, pancakes, toast, or bagels. Refrigerate leftovers.

Makes 1 cup

CHICKEN WITH RASPBERRY SHRUB

A shrub is a mixture of fruit juice, vinegar, sugar, honey, maple syrup, and spices. This recipe comes from the Pennsylvania General Store, which sells shrub mixtures. Its intense flavor livens up a variety of dishes.

Flour, for dredging

4 chicken cutlets, cut into thin strips

2 tablespoons butter

2 tablespoons olive oil

2 celery ribs, thinly sliced

¼ cup raspberry shrub

Freshly ground black pepper to taste

Lightly flour the chicken strips, shaking off excess flour. In a medium skillet, heat butter and oil together until hot. Brown chicken quickly on all sides, about 2 to 3 minutes total. Remove chicken from skillet and set aside.

If necessary, add a little more butter or oil to the skillet. Add celery, and stir-fry for 1 to 2 minutes. Return chicken to skillet, add the shrub, season with black pepper, and cook for 1 to 2 minutes more, or until shrub lightly glazes the chicken.

Makes 4 servings

CHICKEN SALAD SANDWICH

Julie Holahan came up with this sandwich during what she calls her creative 4-H years. It's a favorite among customers of the Reading Terminal Box Lunch.

1 small onion, finely chopped
$\frac{1}{2}$ cup finely chopped celery
$\frac{1}{4}$ cup grated carrot
1 cup grapes
4 cups cubed, cooked chicken

$\frac{1}{2}$ cup mayonnaise
$\frac{1}{4}$ teaspoon freshly ground black pepper
1 teaspoon Old Bay seasoning, or to taste
12 slices bread (any kind)

In a large bowl, combine the onion, celery, carrot, grapes, and chicken. Gradually add the mayonnaise. Season with pepper and Old Bay. Divide the mixture into 6 portions and make 6 sandwiches using the 12 slices of bread.

Makes 6 sandwiches

Market customer: Marge Nichols

Marge Nichols has called the Philadelphia area home since 1974, and she has regularly shopped at Reading Terminal Market. Corporate transfers, however, have taken her to such far-flung places as The Netherlands, Indonesia, Hong Kong, Boston, Florida, and Louisiana. Each place has exposed her to unique regional and ethnic cuisines, and as an avid cook, she has taken advantage of her travels to learn about the techniques and styles of these places. Now back in the Philadelphia area, she is again a regular patron of the market. She most appreciates the quality, freshness, and diversity of its wares.

For this recipe, she buys many ingredients at The Spice Terminal.

Roast Chicken with Yogurt Masala

3 tablespoons plain yogurt

3 to 4 cloves garlic, minced

2 teaspoons minced ginger root

1/8 teaspoon red food coloring

1 teaspoon dried coriander

2 teaspoons cumin powder

1 tablespoon lemon juice

2 pounds chicken parts, skinned, washed, and dried

1/4 teaspoon garam masala (see note)

1 teaspoon salt, or to taste

Butter, for baking

Lemon slices, for garnish

Chutney, for garnish

Sliced onions, for garnish

Preheat oven to 350° F. Make the marinade by mixing together in a large bowl the yogurt, garlic, ginger, food coloring, coriander, cumin, and lemon juice. Place chicken parts in the marinade, covering all parts well. Let sit in the refrigerator for 4 to 5 hours, or overnight. Remove from refrigerator about 30 minutes before cooking.

Place chicken parts in a frying pan, and cook for about 10 minutes, turning once, to dry the excess liquids. Remove from heat, and sprinkle chicken with garam masala and salt. Place chicken on top of buttered foil on a baking sheet, and dab each piece with a bit of butter. Bake for 20 to 25 minutes. Serve with lemon slices, chutney, and sliced onion.

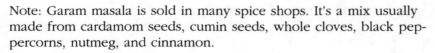

Note: Garam masala is sold in many spice shops. It's a mix usually made from cardamom seeds, cumin seeds, whole cloves, black peppercorns, nutmeg, and cinnamon.

Makes 4 servings

CHAPTER 4 *The Produce Stands*

Recent years have seen a newfound interest in vegetables, marked by an improvement in quality and an increased variety of local and imported produce. At the produce stands in the market, you'll find far more than the standard supermarket selection: fresh cranberry beans; haricots verts, the slender French beans; broccoli rabe; daikon; and many different cabbages, including bok choy and savoy. In the summer, look for mounds of local corn and tomatoes, wonderful juicy peaches, apricots, and nectarines, all mingling with strawberries, blueberries, and raspberries. And year round you can buy cultivated "wild" mushrooms, such as porcini, shiitake, oyster, and crimini. And all during the spring, summer, and fall, the homegrown fruits and vegetables from Pennsylvania's Lancaster County are lavishly displayed for customers.

Mounds of vegetables and fruits are displayed in abundance at Iovine, run by Jimmy and Vinnie Iovine, which has developed a market for Hispanic vegetables. So you can now find yucca plants, plantains, red Cuban bananas, and jicama. And there are some unusual offerings, too – calabaza, for example, similar to a large melon but less watery; and chayote, a crisp member of the squash family. Iovine has also devoted itself to carrying an extensive selection of fresh and dried mushrooms – from portobello, a dense, meaty and frequently large mushroom, to the more delicate chanterelle and oyster mushrooms. Containers of dried morels, chanterelles, wood ear, and porcini are also carried.

O.K. Lee, a family-run produce business, carries a fine variety of fruits and vegetables and an extensive range of Asian produce, including tofu, fresh bean

A well-stocked produce stall, mid-1900s.

sprouts, Chinese cabbages, and dried black Chinese mushrooms. The stand is the namesake of its owner and carries many other Asian ingredients, too, including cans of black bean sauce, plum sauce, straw mushrooms, bamboo shoots, vinegars, and oils.

John's Vegetable Garden, owned by John Brown, came into the market in the summer of 1996. His elongated stand carries many different fruits and vegetables, all attractively displayed.

The year-round stands are joined during the summer months by others. Earl Livingood and Benuel Kauffman, organic farmers from Lancaster County, and Whitney Scott, all display their homegrown beets, squash, tomatoes, and other summer favorites. And Lester Halteman, though primarily a game merchant, also sells seasonal produce.

Market customer: Fabian Cortez

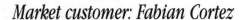

Fabian Cortez, a native Philadelphian, comes to the market not only to see his cousin, Michael Holahan, who owns the Pennsylvania General Store, but also to shop. He enjoys cooking and gave us this recipe, which he says was passed on to him by Mary Sorrentino, a good friend who grew up in Philadelphia's Germantown section, and was a frequent shopper at the market, but who has now left the area. She enjoyed cooking, and her employees at the hardware store she owned also enjoyed her dishes. She would leave them at work while she shopped at the market. She had a kitchen on the premises and would cook for them with the food she brought back from the market. This dish was one of the most popular. Cortez recalls her saying that this "was a Depression kind of dish" – meaning that it was cheap, tasty, and filling.

SAVOY CABBAGE AND BEANS

Olive oil

About 4 ounces fatback or pancetta, diced

2 cloves garlic, chopped

2 heads savoy cabbage, sliced

1/2 cup water

2 19-ounce cans white kidney beans

Salt and freshly ground black pepper to taste

1 teaspoon crushed red pepper flakes

Cover the bottom of a large, heavy saucepan with oil. Add fatback or pancetta, and brown until crisp. Do not drain. Add garlic, and sauté for about 1 minute. Add cabbage and water. Stir and cover. Cook until cabbage is tender, about 15 minutes. Do not overcook. Add beans with their liquid, stir, and season with salt and pepper. Add crushed red pepper, return to heat, and simmer until beans have heated through.

Makes 4 to 6 servings

BAKED FENNEL

Fennel is delicious eaten raw in a salad or dipped in olive oil as Italians like it, but Al Starzi of The Spice Terminal suggests cooking it. Slow cooking brings out fennel's characteristic sweet anise flavor that goes so well with many roasts and game dishes.

4 bulbs fennel, sliced in half, each half cut into thin slices

1 cup fresh basil, chopped, or 1 tablespoon dried

5 tablespoons olive oil

Preheat oven to 350° F. Place fennel slices on a baking sheet, sprinkle the basil over the fennel, and drizzle with olive oil, tossing lightly to coat the fennel. Bake, covered with foil, for 15 minutes. Uncover and cook for 15 minutes more, or until fennel is tender. Serve hot or at room temperature.

Makes 4 to 6 servings

WILD MUSHROOM STUFFING

This can be used as a stuffing before baking pork, chicken, or veal, or it can be baked separately as a side dish. Thoroughly cleaning mushrooms is important, but they absorb water like a sponge, so don't soak them in water. Instead, gently brush the dirt away with a damp paper towel. If they are full of sand, rinse them quickly but make sure you dry them well. Store mushrooms in a paper bag or ceramic container; kept in plastic, they will turn mushy. Morels are dark brown with a nutlike taste. Chanterelles are trumpet-shaped with a light, delicate flavor. Oyster mushrooms are beige with mild flavor. Porcini and portobellos are large and brown with a meaty, smoky flavor. Shiitake are tawny with flat caps and a rich, nutty taste. Use Iovine's wonderful mushroom selection for this dish.

$1/4$ pound (1 stick) butter

$1^1/_2$ pounds fresh wild mushrooms (such as morels, shiitakes, chanterelles, oysters, porcini, or portobellos), sliced

1 cup minced onion

1 cup minced celery

2 cups bread cubes

1 tablespoon minced fresh sage

$1/_2$ tablespoon minced fresh marjoram

$1^1/_2$ teaspoons salt

1 teaspoon pepper

Preheat oven to 325° F. Grease a $2^1/_2$-quart casserole.

Melt the butter in a large skillet over low heat. Add the mushrooms, onion, and celery, and sauté for about 5 minutes. Remove from heat. Add the bread cubes, sage, marjoram, salt, and pepper, mixing to coat well. Let sit to absorb juices.

Place mushroom mixture into the prepared casserole and bake for 1 hour in the preheated oven.

Makes 4 servings

BAKED PLANTAINS

A plantain is a banana with a brownish skin, but it is often used as a vegetable. Plantains are ideal in soups and stews, or baked and served like a baked potato. Slice them and bake or sauté, as in this recipe from Iovine.

4 green plantains $^1/_4$ cup brown sugar

4 tablespoons butter

Preheat oven to 350° F. Peel and halve plantains, soak them in lightly salted water for 30 minutes, drain, and place in a greased baking dish.

Dot the plantains with half the butter, and sprinkle with half the brown sugar. Bake, uncovered, for 20 to 25 minutes, turn, dot again with remaining butter and sugar, and cook for another 25 to 30 minutes, or until plantains are tender.

Makes 4 servings

JICAMA SALAD

Jicama is similar to an apple in that it has a crunchy sweetness. When buying jicama, Jimmy and Vinnie Iovine advise picking fruit that is smooth-skinned and unbruised. They also keep in the refrigerator for two to three weeks.

2 medium-sized jicama (about $1\frac{1}{2}$ pounds)

$\frac{3}{4}$ cup fresh orange juice

1 tablespoon fresh lime juice

1 teaspoon salt

1 tablespoon chopped fresh cilantro

1 large navel orange, peeled and separated into sections

Peel jicama and slice into strips. In a medium bowl, combine orange juice, lime juice, salt, and cilantro. Cover and refrigerate for 1 hour to blend flavors. Add jicama to marinade and stir to coat. Place orange sections on a plate, alternating with slices of jicama. Drizzle any remaining juice over slices. Serve.

Makes 2 servings

Mu-shu Vegetables

Traditionally, mu-shu vegetables would be served with pancakes, but the vegetables are good with rice, too, says David Maw from The Golden Bowl. He makes this vegetable dish with ingredients that he buys at the market and notes that this recipe produces a fairly dry result.

1½ tablespoons oyster sauce

1 teaspoon soy paste

1 teaspoon sesame oil

1 teaspoon Chinese cooking sherry

1 teaspoon hoisin sauce

2 tablespoons vegetable oil

1 egg, beaten

1 clove garlic, minced

6 to 8 dried black mushrooms, softened in hot water for 30 minutes

½ cup shredded bamboo shoots

½ pound mushrooms, sliced

1 cup shredded cabbage (less than 1 small head)

1 carrot, shredded

2 scallions, chopped

In a bowl, combine half the oyster sauce, soy paste, sesame oil, sherry, and hoisin sauce. Mix thoroughly and set aside.

In a skillet or wok, heat the oil, pour in the egg, and, with a spatula, turn the egg until it resembles scrambled eggs. Add the garlic and remaining oyster sauce. Add the black mushrooms, bamboo shoots, sliced mushrooms, cabbage, and carrot, and stir-fry rapidly for 2 to 3 minutes, or until the vegetables have wilted. Pour in the reserved sauce mixture, toss with the vegetables, and stir-fry another 30 seconds. Sprinkle with scallions, and serve with rice.

Makes 2 servings

HERBED POLENTA WITH SUN-DRIED TOMATOES

Polenta is made from both white and yellow corn and can be coarse, medium, or fine. Depending on the dish, polenta can be cooked in water, milk, or broth, and its texture can vary from soft to thick. This dish, from former market merchants Michael Brown and his brother, Steven, can be served as an appetizer or as part of a main course.

1 large onion, chopped

4 cloves garlic, chopped

2 tablespoons olive oil

1 bunch fresh basil, leaves only, chopped

$5\frac{1}{2}$ cups water

Pinch of salt

4 ounces sun-dried tomatoes (loose, not oil-packed)

$1\frac{1}{2}$ cups cornmeal

Grated Parmesan cheese to taste

In a medium skillet over low heat, gently sauté the onion and garlic in the olive oil for about 10 minutes until onion has softened. Add basil and continue to simmer over low heat for 5 minutes, stirring occasionally.

Place the water in a large saucepan, add the salt as the water comes to a boil, then add the sun-dried tomatoes, cover, and cook gently for 2 minutes. Slowly add the cornmeal to the water, stirring constantly with a whisk.

Reduce heat to a simmer and, using a wooden spoon, continue stirring for about 10 minutes. Then add in the onion and garlic mixture. If the mixture seems too thick, add a little more water, and continue to simmer for another 15 minutes. Serve the polenta soft as a side dish, dolloped on a plate, or pour it into a 10 x 10-inch baking dish and allow to cool. When cool, cut into squares, top with some Parmesan cheese, and reheat in a 350° F. oven.

Makes 4 servings

BAKED EGGPLANT

With the wide variety of vinegars available today, the opportunity to experiment with different flavors and to add zest and pungency to many dishes is nearly limitless. Vinegars will keep almost indefinitely if kept tightly sealed after opening and if stored in a cool, dark place. This recipe is based on a suggestion from John's Vegetable Garden.

1 pound plum tomatoes, sliced	3 tablespoons raspberry vinegar
2 cups chopped fresh basil	$\frac{1}{2}$ cup olive oil
4 cloves garlic, minced	2 medium or 6 Italian eggplants, cut into $\frac{1}{2}$-inch strips
Salt and freshly ground pepper to taste	8 ounces feta cheese, crumbled

Preheat oven to 325° F. Place tomatoes on a baking sheet and bake for 1 hour until slightly shriveled. Remove and let cool. Turn on the broiler to preheat it.

Place basil, garlic, salt, pepper, and vinegar into a food processor, and, with the motor running, gradually add the oil. The consistency should be fairly runny. Add more oil if necessary.

Place strips of eggplant on a baking sheet, brush with the oil mixture, broil for 2 to 3 minutes under the preheated broiler, turn, and broil strips on the other side.

In a medium baking dish, layer half the eggplant strips on the bottom, cover with half the dried tomato, and sprinkle with half the feta. Add a second layer of eggplant, the remaining tomato, any leftover basil oil mixture, and the remaining feta. Cover with foil and bake for 30 minutes, remove foil, and broil until brown on top.

Makes 4 servings

STIR-FRIED CHINESE CABBAGE

Chinese cabbage, sometimes called bok choy, is a white-stalked, green-leafed cabbage with a slightly bitter taste. If cooked quickly, it retains its crispness and mellow flavor. This recipe is from O.K. Lee.

2 heads bok choy (about 1½ pounds), washed thoroughly

3 tablespoons vegetable oil

A 1-inch slice of gingerroot, peeled and chopped

1 clove garlic, chopped

1 tablespoon water

1 tablespoon rice wine vinegar

Pinch salt

2 teaspoons sesame oil

Trim the stem ends from the bok choy, removing any tough pieces. Cut the leaves and stems into 1-inch slices, and keep them separate.

Over high heat, heat a wok or skillet, add the oil, toss in the ginger and garlic, and stir-fry for about 5 seconds. Add the sliced bok choy stems, and toss over high heat for a few seconds. Add the water, cover and cook about 1 minute. Add the sliced bok choy leaves, the vinegar, and the salt. Stir-fry over high heat for about 45 seconds, or until the leaves have wilted. Drizzle with sesame oil. Serve hot or at room temperature.

Makes 4 servings

Market customers: Otto and Nury Reichert

Otto and Nury Reichert met in New York and arrived in Philadelphia in 1958. Otto was born in northern Germany; Nury is from Barcelona, Spain. Otto discovered his love of Spanish cooking while taking many vacations in Spain with his wife and children. Since his retirement, he has taken an interest in cooking, and he often drives to Reading Terminal Market from his home in Philadelphia's Roxborough section and makes a day of it. He enjoys talking to the merchants while eating lunch and shopping for the week. This recipe combines his love of fish with his fondness for Spanish cooking.

OTTO'S BULLABESA CATALANA

$1/4$ cup olive oil

3 ribs celery, finely chopped

1 medium onion, finely chopped

1 clove garlic, finely chopped

1 scallion, finely chopped

1 teaspoon dried thyme, or 1 tablespoon fresh

1 bay leaf

1 28-ounce can crushed tomatoes

3 8-ounce bottles clam juice

1 cup dry white wine

2 tablespoons fresh parsley, minced

1 bulb fennel, finely chopped

Salt and freshly ground pepper to taste

1 pound whitefish, monkfish, cod, or flounder, cut in chunks

$1/2$ pound medium shrimp, shelled

$3/4$ pound bay scallops

Heat the oil in a large saucepan, and sauté the celery, onion, garlic, scallion, thyme, and bay leaf in the hot oil over medium heat for about 15 minutes, stirring frequently. Add the tomatoes, clam juice, wine, parsley, fennel, salt, and pepper, and simmer 15 minutes longer.

Add fish chunks, shrimp, and scallops to the soup, and simmer about 5 minutes, or until fish is opaque and shrimp and scallops are cooked through. Serve with a salad.

Makes 6 to 8 servings

A successful seafood dinner requires, above all, starting with the freshest fish or shellfish available. And there's no better place to do this than at Reading Terminal Market, which offers an extensive variety of whole fish, fillets, shellfish, and farm-raised fish from around the country and the world.

You'll find red snapper from Florida and the Caribbean, rockfish from Maryland, mountain trout from Connecticut, scrod from Maine, sashimi tuna from Hawaii, St. Peter's fish from Israel, and salmon from Norway and Canada. Local and seasonal fish, such as shad in the spring and soft-shell crabs in the summer, are offered at the three fish stalls that grace the market.

"Eat fish and live longer" proclaims the sign above John Yi Fish, one of the three. Owners Suzi Kim and her husband, John Yi, offer suggestions on how to cook fish. Their usual suggestion: Very simply. A few years ago they briefly owned Pearl's Oyster Bar before expanding their own fish stall in the market.

Hyun Chang Byun and his wife, Soonrye, arrived in this country from Korea many years ago and opened Byun's Seafood in 1982. Over the years, they have expanded their business to include prepared fish ready to go, such as breaded shrimps, scallops, crabcakes, and fish cakes.

Ms. Kim, as she calls herself and is known to her customers, owns The Golden Bowl Market, the third fish stall at Reading Terminal Market. Shoppers may recall the story of a customer who arrived home and found a substantial

A customer inspects her selection under new fluorescent lighting at a 1940s fish stall.

amount of cash in with the fish. The customer promptly returned the money to The Golden Bowl, and Ms. Kim was equally surprised – and very thankful.

The Korean ownership of the three stands reinforces the diversity of the market, its offerings, and its customers.

Monkfish Soup

One fascinating aspect of the market is the exchange of ideas and ingredients between one culture and another. The Korean name for this soup is Me Untang, according to Suzi Kim at John Yi's fish stall.

1 pound monkfish or cod, cut into 1-inch chunks

1 teaspoon miso

1 tablespoon soy sauce

1 clove garlic, peeled and crushed

6 cups water

$1/2$ cup kim chee (available prepared at Reading Terminal Market, Asian markets, and many supermarkets)

In a large saucepan, place fish, miso, soy sauce, garlic, and water. Bring to a boil, reduce heat, and simmer for 8 to 10 minutes, or until fish flakes easily. Add kim chee to soup, simmer another 2 to 3 minutes, or until just heated through.

Makes 4 servings

STEAMED RED SNAPPER

This recipe comes from Ms. Kim of the Golden Bowl Market. She says the marinade is equally delicious served over other white fish.

4 red snapper fillets	1 tablespoon oyster sauce
1 teaspoon chopped ginger	$\frac{1}{4}$ cup rice wine vinegar
2 cloves garlic, chopped	$\frac{1}{2}$ teaspoon hot pepper sauce

Place fish fillets in a shallow pan. In a bowl, combine remaining ingredients, pour over fish, and let marinate in the refrigerator for 1 to 2 hours. Remove fish from marinade and place in a steamer. Pour some of the marinade over the fish and let steam for about 5 minutes, or until fish is firm and opaque. Boil remaining marinade in a small saucepan, about 5 minutes. Place fish on a platter and top with heated sauce.

Makes 4 servings

SAUTÉED SOFT-SHELL CRABS

Soft-shell crabs are an East Coast delicacy, generally available from June to September. When buying soft-shells, whether they are still alive or already cleaned, make sure they are indeed soft and pliable – not leathery or semi-hard. Soft-shells freeze well if cleaned, patted dry, and wrapped securely in plastic wrap or foil. To defrost, place crabs in the refrigerator overnight. Soft-shells are very watery, so gently pat them dry with a paper towel before cooking.

8 soft-shell crabs, cleaned and patted dry

Cornstarch, for dredging

Olive oil, for sautéeing

Grated zest and juice of 2 limes

¼ cup white wine or dry vermouth

Salt and freshly ground pepper to taste

Dredge crabs lightly in the cornstarch, shaking off any excess.

Coat the bottom of a large skillet with olive oil, and heat oil until hot. Sauté the crabs for about 5 minutes on each side, or until well-crisped. Remove from pan and keep warm.

Add lime zest, lime juice, and wine or vermouth to the skillet, deglazing the skillet by scraping up the browned bits with a wooden spoon. Season with salt and pepper. Serve crabs drizzled with liquid from the skillet.

Makes 4 servings

Market customer: David Ludwig

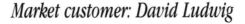

Though he is a relative newcomer to Philadelphia, David Ludwig, a freelance writer, quickly discovered Reading Terminal Market, which reminded him of food markets in Europe. He enjoys shopping at Reading Terminal Market because "it is a source for good-quality and interesting ingredients needed for preparing all kinds of dishes." The following recipe is based on a soup he had at a tapas bar in the Spanish town of Jerez.

SCALLOPS WITH TOMATO AND PAPRIKA SAUCE

4 tablespoons butter

1 pound scallops, cut in half horizontally if large

Salt and freshly ground pepper to taste

$1/4$ cup cognac

1 cup tomato sauce

1 teaspoon paprika

1 clove garlic, chopped

1 teaspoon finely chopped parsley

2 tablespoons grated Gruyère, Parmesan, or a combination

Additional butter, for baking

Preheat oven to 450° F. Heat 2 tablespoons of the butter in a large skillet, and add the scallops. Season with salt and pepper. Cook about 2 minutes, occasionally shaking the skillet to prevent from sticking.

Heat the cognac for 20 to 30 seconds in a small saucepan, ignite very carefully with a match, and pour flaming liquid over the scallops, shaking the pan until the flames subside. Cook for about 1 minute. Add the tomato sauce, paprika, garlic, and parsley. Cook for another 2 minutes.

Spoon equal amounts of the mixture into 4 ramekins or a baking dish. Sprinkle with cheese, dot with butter on top, and bake in the oven for about 8 minutes.

Makes 4 servings

ORANGE ROUGHY WITH LEMON MARINADE

Suzi Kim of John Yi Fish prefers simplicity in fish cookery, which is evident in the following recipe. Other types of white fish, such as flounder, can be substituted.

Juice of ¹⁄₂ lemon
Zest of 1 lemon
2 teaspoons Dijon mustard
2 tablespoons olive oil

4 orange roughy fillets, about 1¹⁄₂ pounds total
Salt and freshly ground pepper to taste
¹⁄₂ pound snow peas, trimmed

Preheat oven to 350° F. In a small bowl, whisk together lemon juice, lemon zest, and mustard. Gradually add oil until well blended. Lightly oil a baking pan, place fish in one layer, season with salt and pepper, and pour marinade on top.

Cover the fish with foil and bake for approximately 5 minutes. Remove foil and continue baking for another 5 minutes, or until the fish is opaque.

While fish is baking, bring a saucepan of water to a boil, plunge in the snow peas, and blanch for about 20 seconds. Drain peas, and serve beside the fish.

Makes 4 servings

BROILED SHAD WITH HERBS

One of the first signs of spring at the market – and at John Yi's fish stand – is the appearance of shad. This fast-moving fish migrates with the seasons, and the start of shad season in the Philadelphia area is celebrated annually at the Lambertville Shad Festival in New Jersey. Shad is a rich fish with a soft flesh and fine texture, lending itself to baking, broiling, or grilling.

2 boneless shad fillets, each about 1 pound

¼ cup olive oil

Juice of 1 lemon

⅓ cup white wine or dry vermouth

1 tablespoon herbes de Provence

Salt and freshly ground pepper to taste

Lemon wedges, for garnish

Place shad skin side down in a shallow, ovenproof pan large enough to hold the fillets in one layer. In a bowl, mix together the olive oil, lemon juice, wine or vermouth, herbes de Provence, salt, and pepper. Brush the fish liberally with this mixture.

Place fish under a preheated broiler, and cook for 6 to 8 minutes, basting once or twice with the oil mixture. When fillets are opaque and flake easily with a fork, they are done. Pour any juices that have accumulated in the pan over the fish and adjust seasonings. Garnish with lemon and serve.

Makes 4 servings

SAUTÉED SHAD ROE

Shad roe is delicate and rich-tasting. Preparing roe simply and serving it with a light sauce is one of the best ways to enjoy it. Placing the roe in warm water for a few minutes will help keep it firm and intact during cooking. Shad roe is available from any of the fish merchants, and this recipe idea came from a customer who wished to remain anonymous.

2 sets shad roe

Salt and freshly ground pepper to taste

$\frac{1}{2}$ cup flour

$\frac{1}{4}$ pound (1 stick) unsalted butter

1 tablespoon olive oil

$\frac{1}{3}$ cup white wine or dry vermouth

Juice of 1 lemon

1 teaspoon champagne mustard or Dijon mustard

2 tablespoons chopped fennel leaves

Dip roe into warm water and let sit for a few minutes. Drain and pat dry with paper towel. Separate the lobes by gently removing the membrane between them. Sprinkle with salt and pepper. Dredge in flour and gently shake off the excess.

In a skillet, melt 6 tablespoons of the butter with the oil. When the mixture begins to foam, reduce the heat, gently add the roe, and cook for about 5 to 6 minutes on each side. Carefully transfer to a warm platter and set aside.

In the skillet, add the remaining 2 tablespoons of butter, and stir in the wine or vermouth, lemon juice, mustard, and fennel leaves. Toss gently and heat through. Pour sauce over roe and serve.

Makes 4 servings

CHAPTER 6 .... *The Bakeries*

Philadelphians have long had a deep love affair with good breads and a passion for pastries. Reading Terminal Market has the best of both. Many of the bakeries now in the market began their businesses in other parts of the city and then expanded into the market – much to the delight of the owners, who saw immediate success, and the market customers, who had always been loyal to local products. Reading Terminal Market is now home to some of the best bake shops in the city.

Le Bus, owned by David Braverman, started serving food to University of Pennsylvania students from a converted school bus parked on a West Philadelphia street. It was in that bus that Le Bus baked its first loaf of bread in a small propane oven. Today, Le Bus breads are made and baked in its large, well-equipped bakery in the city's Manayunk section. Breads are traditionally baked on a stone, brick, or tile hearth. To achieve a similar result, David Braverman imported from France a Pavailler hearth oven that produced the right look, color, and texture of breads. One outlet for Le Bus's bread supply is at Reading Terminal Market, where early in the day you'll find on display a variety of freshly baked breads, such as country sourdough, a simple and basic bread with a mellow-sour flavor; Stirato, which is stretched by hand before being baked; Italian and French breads; and a honey and oatmeal bread that contains seven different grains.

Gene and Rosalyn Braverman (no relation to David) are the creative owners of Braverman's, another bakery in the market best known for its internationally inspired selection – French truffles and mousses, Italian tiramisu and cannolis, German linzer tortes and strudels, and Russian rugalach and black bread. The Bravermans also make many all-American favorites, such as carrot cake and New York-style cheesecake. Their European-style breads include Tuscan, Parmesan pesto, and raisin pecan.

Old Post Road has been in the market for many years, and on Fridays and Saturdays you will find Hans Stulz setting up his stand with freshly baked cakes and pies that his wife, Claudia, helps prepare and bake. It is well worth your while to shop there early in the day, before the most popular items, such as German apple cake, seasonal fruit pies, shortcakes, and linzer tortes, all disappear. During the summer, the strawberry tarts are exquisite, light, delicate, and mouthwatering.

As you wait in line by Metropolitan Bakery, this sign greets you: "The staff of urban life, from Tuscan berry bread, to a cracked wheat sourdough that just won't quit at Metropolitan Bakery." That describes the business. Metropolitan Bakery, a recent addition to the market, is owned by Wendy Smith Born and James Barrett. They have created an excellent business for themselves, and their wide variety of breads piled high in attractive baskets are always gone by day's end. Barrett, whose workday begins at night, bakes bread very traditionally, using only natural starters. Willow baskets are used to mold and proof each loaf of bread, which Barrett says also gives the bread a unique taste and texture. An unusual focaccia with a potato topping is very addictive, as are the muffins, scones, cookies, and pies.

Termini Bros. Bakery, a family-owned business since 1921, is one of Philadelphia's best-known and oldest Italian bakeries. Owner Vincent Termini, who opened his business in the market in 1984, has followed the family custom of preparing authentic Italian pastries. All the pastries are prepared in Termini's flagship store located near South Philadelphia's Italian Market. The store was founded by Vincent's father, Giuseppe. Termini's popularity has spread, and it now ships tinned, handmade Italian cookies nationwide. The store offers cannolis, biscotti, cakes, cookies, and seasonal pies, all displayed behind cases that seem to stretch on forever.

The story of the Famous 4th Street Cookie began at the 4th Street Deli, owned by David Auspitz. For years, the store sold only one brand of ice cream, but when Auspitz started carrying another brand, the first manufacturer ripped out the freezer, leaving a large hole. David's wife, Janie, wanted to use the space to sell her cookies. Since then, they have become Philadelphia favorites. Reading Terminal Market has enjoyed the results and now sells many varieties of her cookies. Scoops of cookie dough sit on baking trays in view of passersby, ready to go into the oven. They come out of the oven too, of course – hot, delicious-smelling, and luscious-looking.

GERMAN APPLE CAKE

Hans Stulz of Old Post Road suggests using a tart apple for this cake.

$^1/_4$ pound (1 stick) butter

$^1/_2$ cup sugar

2 teaspoons vanilla

1 teaspoon lemon extract

3 large eggs

$1^3/_4$ cups all-purpose flour

2 teaspoons baking powder

5 to 6 Rome or Granny Smith apples, depending on size, peeled, cored, and halved

2 tablespoons apricot jam

1 tablespoon water

Whipped cream, for garnish

Preheat oven to 350° F. In a bowl, cream the butter and sugar until well blended. Add vanilla and lemon extracts. Beat in the eggs, one at a time. Sift together the flour and baking powder and add to the butter-egg mixture. Mix until well blended.

The batter will be stiff. Spoon batter into a 10-inch springform pan, and, using a spoon or fork, spread it evenly over the entire bottom of the pan. Cut each apple half into 6 to 8 slices. Starting in the middle of the batter, place the apple slices in concentric circles until the pan is full. Bake for 35 to 45 minutes, or until a cake tester inserted in the middle comes out dry.

Meanwhile, place the apricot jam and water in a small saucepan, and, over low heat, cook until the jam liquefies. Stir until smooth.

When cake is done, let cool for 10 to 15 minutes. Remove from springform pan, and brush top with the apricot mixture. Serve warm or at room temperature with whipped cream.

Makes 6 servings

CORNBREAD LOAF

This bread from Le Bus can be made a day ahead and stored tightly wrapped at room temperature. A quick tip: When mixing quickbreads, combine the wet and dry ingredients until just moistened. Too much mixing will toughen the bread.

$1\frac{1}{2}$ cups all-purpose flour

$1\frac{1}{2}$ cups yellow cornmeal

$\frac{1}{2}$ cup sugar

$\frac{1}{2}$ teaspoon baking powder

$\frac{1}{2}$ teaspoon baking soda

$\frac{1}{2}$ teaspoon salt

2 large eggs

$\frac{1}{2}$ cup vegetable oil

$\frac{1}{2}$ cup milk

$\frac{1}{2}$ cup buttermilk

1 cup corn kernels, fresh or frozen and thawed

Preheat oven to 350° F. Grease a 9 x 5-inch loaf pan, dust pan with cornmeal, and shake out the excess.

Combine the flour, $1\frac{1}{2}$ cups of cornmeal, sugar, baking powder, baking soda, and salt in a large bowl. Whisk the eggs, oil, milk, and buttermilk in a medium bowl. Add egg mixture and the corn to the dry ingredients, and stir just until combined. Pour batter into prepared pan, and bake for 15 minutes. Reduce temperature to 325° F. and continue baking about 1 hour, until a tester inserted into the center of the loaf comes out clean.

Cool bread in the pan on a rack for 30 minutes. Turn out bread onto the rack. Serve warm or at room temperature.

Makes 6 servings

German Chocolate Topping

Diane Braverman says that either sweetened or unsweetened coconut can be used in this recipe, a topping to fill and frost your favorite chocolate cake layers. The coconut adds a creamy texture to the topping, which holds nicely during spreading.

1 cup heavy cream

1 cup sugar

3 egg yolks, lightly beaten

1/4 pound (1 stick) unsalted butter, cut into small pieces

1 teaspoon vanilla extract

2 cups sweetened shredded coconut

1 1/3 cups pecans, coarsely chopped

In a mixing bowl, whisk together the cream, sugar, and egg yolks. In a large, heavy saucepan, melt the butter, stir in the egg mixture and the vanilla, and, over medium-high heat, bring to a boil. Continue boiling for 5 minutes. Stir in the coconut, and reduce the heat to low. Cook 5 minutes more, stirring often. Add the pecans and remove from the heat, stirring occasionally until cool. Cover and keep refrigerated until needed.

Makes enough to fill and frost a 9-inch cake

CHOCOLATE CHIP BISCOTTI WITH ALMONDS

Rosalyn Braverman and daughter Diane Braverman, after much trial and error, finally put together this biscotti recipe that not only pleases them, but friends and relatives too. "These chocolate almond biscotti go terrifically with a cup of espresso, cappuccino, or hot chocolate," Diane said, "and not so well dipped in wine as are the ones made with only ground almonds." She was referring to the Italian tradition of dipping plain biscotti into dry red wine.

2 cups unbleached flour

$1/2$ teaspoon baking powder

$1/2$ teaspoon salt

1 cup minus 1 tablespoon sugar

7 ounces whole almonds, with or without skins

12 ounces semisweet chocolate chips

2 large eggs

1 teaspoon vanilla extract

1 tablespoon almond-flavored liqueur

Position the two oven racks so that the oven is divided into three equal sections, and preheat oven to 375° F. Use cookie sheets lined with parchment paper or foil with the shiny side up. In a large bowl, sift together the flour, baking powder, and salt, then stir in the sugar and mix.

In the workbowl of a food processor, add $1/2$ cup of the dry ingredients and $1/2$ cup of the almonds, and process for 30 seconds, or until a light powder forms. Combine this mixture with the rest of the sifted ingredients, then coarsely chop the remaining nuts and add them to the sifted ingredients along with the chocolate chips.

In another small bowl, beat the eggs with vanilla and the liqueur just enough to mix. Add this mixture to the dry ingredients, stirring to moisten them. Do not overmix.

Working with wet hands and on a large sheet of parchment or wax paper, shape the dough into a long mound. Cut dough into quarters, and, keeping your hands wet, shape each quarter of dough into strips about 10 inches long, $2^1/_2$ inches wide, and $3/_4$ inch high. (Use only your hands, not a rolling pin.) Place dough on the prepared trays, and place the trays on the racks in the oven. Bake for approximately 20 minutes. Midway through the baking, switch the top and bottom trays and rotate front to back.

Remove from oven, slide parchment off the trays, and, using a wide metal spatula, place biscotti on a cutting board. Let cool for 10 to 15 minutes. Reduce oven temperature to 275° F. With a serrated knife, cut at a 45-

degree angle into ¹/₂-inch-wide slices. Cut slowly, using a sawing motion. Place slices cut side down on the two cookie sheets, this time without a lining. Return to oven, and bake for 20 to 25 minutes, again switching trays top and bottom and front to back once. Carefully turn slices (they'll be hot). Turn off oven and leave biscotti there to cool, then store in sealed container.

Makes 40 pieces

METROPOLITAN FOCACCIA

Focaccia is a crusty, flat Italian bread that goes through one rising before being baked. Metropolitan Bakery makes its focaccia with a starter, which is included as an option. An easier way, which is quite acceptable, is to make it with yeast, as this recipe does.

$1\frac{1}{3}$ cups water

$\frac{1}{3}$ cup milk

$\frac{1}{3}$ cup olive oil, plus 1 tablespoon for brushing dough

1 tablespoon yeast

3 cups unbleached flour

1 tablespoon wheat germ

1 teaspoon salt

Semolina, for dusting

In a large bowl, combine 1 cup of the water, milk, olive oil, yeast, flour, and wheat germ. Stir with a wooden spoon to mix (the dough will be quite sticky). Continue stirring for about 5 minutes until the dough comes together and has become elastic. Let dough rest for about 20 minutes, sprinkle the salt on top, and mix into the dough. Add remaining water and continue kneading, using either floured hands or a wooden spoon, for about 4 minutes, until dough is smooth and elastic.

With floured hands, divide the dough into 2 pieces, and shape each into a round or a rectangle. Place on parchment paper and sprinkle the top with semolina. Cover with a cloth, and let rise for 1 hour. The dough should have risen only slightly, and should still be quite spongy.

Preheat oven to 400° F. Brush the top of the dough with olive oil, pinch the surface with your fingers, and bake for 30 minutes, or until the bread is lightly browned and crusty.

Note: This recipe can be made with a starter in place of the yeast. The starter takes advance planning to make and needs to be refreshed to keep it alive (see next page for recipe).

Makes 2 loaves

FOCACCIA STARTER

3 cups filtered water   1 pound black grapes
1 pound organic white bread
flour

Combine the water and flour in a heavy container. Wrap the grapes in cheesecloth and tie into a bundle. Pound the cloth to smash the grapes, and submerge in the water-flour mixture. Cover and leave in a cool, dry place for at least 48 hours (72 is preferable).

Gently stir the mixture and discard half of it. Refresh the remainder with a mixture of 1 cup water and 2 cups flour. Stir, cover, and let sit for another 24 hours. Again, stir, discard half, and refresh with another mixture of 1 cup water and 2 cups flour.

This will leave you with an active, thin starter with a freshly sour aroma that is ready to use in your favorite bread recipe.

Refresh the starter by replacing what you have used with a mixture of 1 part water and 2 parts flour. Refrigerate the starter and feed it at least once a week with a mixture of 1 part water and 2 parts flour. If you use the starter more often, feed it as you use it.

NOODLE PUDDING

Janie Auspitz of The Famous 4th Street Cookie Co. would not give out any cookie recipes. But she was more than happy to give a recipe for noodle pudding, taken from her mother's handwritten collection. Janie remembers her working in the kitchen making different desserts and trying them out on her. Her mother went to the "a little this, a little that" school of cooking.

6 ounces capellini

$1/_4$ pound (1 stick) butter

$2^1/_2$ tablespoons sugar

4 ounces cream cheese, softened and broken into pieces

3 eggs, beaten

2 cups milk

Cinnamon and sugar, for sprinkling

Preheat oven to 350° F. Grease an 8 x 8-inch baking dish. In a large saucepan, cook noodles in lightly salted water until al dente. Drain, but do not rinse. Melt the butter in a small saucepan. Pour half the melted butter into the drained noodles along with the cream cheese. Mix, sprinkle in the sugar, and mix again.

Place the noodles in a greased baking dish, and mix in the remaining butter. Beat the eggs with the milk, pour over the noodle mixture, sprinkle with cinnamon and sugar, and bake for 45 to 60 minutes, until cooked.

Makes 4 servings

TERMINI'S CHOCOLATE MOUSSE WITH RUM

This mousse is made at Termini Bros., and Barbara Termini, Vincent's wife, makes sure she takes some home for her own dinner parties.

8 ounces semisweet chocolate

2 tablespoons butter, at room temperature

4 eggs, separated

$\frac{1}{4}$ cup light or dark rum

1 cup heavy cream

Melt the chocolate in the top of a double boiler over barely simmering water. Whisk in the butter, then the egg yolks, one at a time. Whisk in the rum. Remove from heat. If the mousse binds up, add more rum until it becomes smooth.

In a separate bowl, whip the egg whites with a balloon whisk or piano-wire whisk until they hold a soft shape. Stir a third of the beaten egg whites into the mousse, then fold in the remaining whites. In the same bowl, whip the cream to a soft peak, and fold it into the mousse. Refrigerate for several hours before serving.

Makes 8 servings

CHAPTER 7 *The Pennsylvania Dutch Merchants*

Pennsylvania's heartland arrived at Reading Terminal Market in 1981, when David O'Neil, then the market's general manager, actually went out to Lancaster County, an hour-plus drive away, to personally persuade some of the local Amish and Mennonite merchants to open businesses in Reading Terminal Market.

They did. The first four stands to open were Dienner's Bar-B-Q Chicken, Esh Eggs and Deli, Glick's Salad, and Fisher's Soft Pretzels and Ice Cream. Now, an entire corner of the market bustles with country-fresh produce and Pennsylvania Dutch specialties. The stands are family-owned and -operated, and many of the merchants are related.

For any first-time visitor to Reading Terminal Market, a stop at Fisher's is almost mandatory. The lines for the pretzels are long, but the wait is entertaining as you watch women in traditional Pennsylvania Dutch dress roll the dough and twist it into its final pretzel shape. You can also watch the pretzels going into the oven, coming out, then being brushed with butter, or perhaps, in the style of the Philadelphia soft pretzel, with a squeeze of mustard or cheese. Fisher's also makes its own ice cream floats, milk shakes, root beer sodas, and waffles with a choice of toppings. On the other side of the pretzel counter, also owned by Levi Fisher, is a candy store, which sells a variety of chocolate-covered and hard candies, nuts, and dried fruits, some colorfully displayed in old-fashioned glass jars. This is truly a childhood fantasy place.

The Dutch Eating Place, run by Sam Esh, opened in 1990. It's comfort food

Members of an Amish family work at their stall in the mid-1980s.

David Esh's stall showcases a variety of his farm-fresh eggs (Burk Uzzle).

at its best, always served with a smile. The Dutch Eating Place is best known for its enormous pancakes, blueberry or plain, served with a side of turkey bacon. Its french toast is made using fresh raisin bread from nearby Beiler's Bakery. The dining counter encircles the kitchen space, so you can watch as the hearty home-made bean and ham soup, chicken-corn soup, and chili are ladled out. "Our mashed potatoes are also real popular," Esh says, "made right from the spud." Other traditional favorites include chicken pot pie and hot apple dumplings served with heavy cream.

At Hatfield Farms Lancaster County Lunch Meats & Cheese, owned by David Esh (a very distant cousin of Sam Esh), thinly sliced Lancaster County lunch meats and cheeses are heaped in mounds in the deli cases. Some of the best sellers include corned beef, pepper ham, and Lebanon bologna. Many shoppers make a special trip here just for the olive loaf and the liver pudding, or for the old-fashioned tub butter. The Dutch Kountry Sandwich Korner, a part of the business, sells sandwiches at a counter.

Glick's Salad, run by Michelle Glick Fetter, features a delightful display of homemade preserves, jellies, and relishes covered with lace-trimmed cotton tops. And entrée items like macaroni and cheese, tapioca and rice puddings, and fresh-ly prepared salads are sold by the pound for takeout. Glick's carries two potato salads: yellow, made with mayonnaise and mustard, and white, which has no sugar added. Fetter talked about several desserts that "are a cross between a cheesecake and pudding" – in that they taste like cheesecake but are scooped up for serving like a pudding. The variety includes cheese delight and black forest cheesecake pudding.

Amish women make fresh pretzels during a 1987 Pennsylvania Dutch Festival at the market (Burk Uzzle).

For either takeout or eating in the market, Dienner's Bar-B-Q Chicken may be the juiciest in town, served with or without Dienner's special hot sauce. Gideon Dienner, the father of the current owner, Sam Dienner, originally owned several businesses in the market. He sold two of them to his sons and one, Beiler's Bakery, to his daughter and son-in-law. Dienner's sells cooked whole or half chickens and chicken wings, all basted with its own seasoning and served with hot dinner rolls and coleslaw.

Across the way is the Lancaster County Dairy, also owned by Sam Esh. Direct from Lancaster County, he brings in white and chocolate milks, light and thick heavy cream, and fresh apple cider in season.

Beiler's Bakery, operated by Alvin Beiler, showcases homemade sticky buns and dinner rolls, all made on the premises. The pastries, cakes, and pies come in fresh from a Mennonite bakery in Lancaster County. The shelves are filled with chocolate eclairs, lemon meringue pies, cream pies, and the Pennsylvania Dutch standard, shoofly pie.

Phares Glick, Michelle Glick Fetter's cousin, owns The Rib Stand and sells both baby-back and regular ribs accompanied by a selection of vegetable side courses, such as barbecued roasted potatoes, baked macaroni and cheese, and coleslaw. Not to be missed is a delectable rib sandwich served on a club roll with hot or mild barbecue sauce.

One of the most interesting shops along the way is Esh Egg Farm, run by David Esh. On display are eggs of every variety and size – brown and white chicken eggs; duck and goose eggs; enormous ostrich, rhea, and emu eggs; as well as tiny quail eggs. The rhea and emu eggs are for ornamental rather than culinary use. In fact, one woman who frequents the market likes to hand-paint designs on them; another customer actually carves them using a fine blade. Adjoining is a stand specializing in fresh turkey products, including turkey sausage, turkey bacon, and turkey kielbasa links.

If you plan to come to the market to see the Pennsylvania Dutch section, be aware that it is open only Wednesday through Saturday, with an early closing on Wednesday.

COLE SLAW

This is a popular side dish served by Phares Glick with the barbecued rib sandwich from The Rib Stand.

1 small head green cabbage, shredded

2 carrots, grated

1 tablespoon sugar

1 tablespoon vegetable oil

2 tablespoons red-wine vinegar or cider vinegar

$1/2$ teaspoon ground celery seed

Salt and freshly ground pepper to taste

1 cup mayonnaise

Place the shredded cabbage in a medium bowl, and add the grated carrot, sugar, oil, vinegar, celery seed, salt, and pepper. Squeeze by hand to extract and blend the juices. Add the mayonnaise and mix thoroughly. Chill for 1 to 2 hours before serving.

Makes 6 servings

CHICKEN POT PIE

When the Pennsylvania Dutch speak of "pot pies," they are referring to large squares of egg noodles, not to the dishes covered with a baked pastry crust that most people associate with the term. The noodle squares are made with flour and eggs and are sold at Esh Eggs. The bouillon cubes are used because they already contain the desired flavorings.

6 cups water

6 chicken bouillon cubes

2 tablespoons butter

1 potato (any variety), peeled and cut into $\frac{1}{2}$-inch cubes

2 carrots, thinly sliced

2 ribs celery, thinly sliced

1 small onion, thinly sliced

Salt and freshly ground pepper to taste

$\frac{1}{2}$ pound pot pie noodles

2 cups cooked chicken (light or dark), skinned, boned, and cut into 1-inch cubes

Boil the water in a large saucepan, and add the bouillon cubes. Stir until cubes have dissolved. Reduce heat to medium-low, and add the butter, potato, carrot, celery, onion, salt, and pepper.

Add the noodles, pushing them down into the broth with a spoon. Cover and cook over low heat until noodles are done, about 25 minutes. Add the chicken and continue cooking 10 minutes longer. Adjust seasoning. Ladle into soup bowls, and serve.

Makes 6 servings

SHOOFLY PIE

Shoofly pie is a well-known Pennsylvania Dutch recipe. Its main ingredient is molasses, once known as "poor man's sugar." Legend has it that the sweetness of the pie attracted flies, which then had to be "shooed" away. Many Amish eat this pie at breakfast. This recipe comes from Beiler's Bakery.

Pastry crust for a 9-inch pie plate, from a standard recipe or storebought

1 teaspoon baking soda

1 cup warm water

1 egg, beaten

1 cup molasses

$1\frac{1}{2}$ cups flour

$\frac{1}{2}$ cup brown sugar

$\frac{1}{2}$ cup shortening

Preheat oven to 425° F. Line a 9-inch pie plate with pastry crust. In a medium bowl, dissolve the baking soda in the water, then mix in the egg and molasses. Place the flour, sugar, and shortening in another bowl, and mix until crumbly. Mix $\frac{1}{2}$ cup of the crumb mixture into the molasses mixture, stir, and pour into the prepared pie shell. Sprinkle the remaining crumbs evenly over the top.

Bake for 15 minutes, reduce heat to 350° F., and bake for 30 minutes more, or until the center of the pie is firm.

Makes 1 9-inch pie

CHICKEN AND CORN SOUP

This soup is especially good when local corn is available. The mixture of flour and egg, when dropped in pieces into the finished soup, forms dumplings that float to the top when they're cooked. This is a version of a soup served at the Dutch Eating Place.

1 chicken, 3 to 4 pounds

1 medium onion, diced

2 ribs celery, diced

3 medium potatoes (any variety), cubed

1 carrot, diced

$\frac{1}{4}$ cup fresh parsley, chopped

4 cups fresh or frozen corn

Salt and freshly ground pepper to taste

1 cup flour

1 egg

$\frac{1}{2}$ cup milk

Place the chicken in a large stockpot and add enough water to cover. Bring to a boil, reduce heat to a simmer, and cook until chicken is tender, about 1 hour. Remove chicken from the water and let cool. Remove skin, cut meat away from the bones, and cut the meat into 1-inch dice.

Let the broth cool, skim off any fat, and strain the broth. In a large saucepan, bring 8 cups of the broth to a boil, add the onion, celery, potato, and carrot. Simmer, covered, for 30 minutes, add the parsley and corn, and continue cooking until the vegetables are tender, about 15 minutes. Add the diced chicken, salt, and pepper.

In a small bowl, combine the flour, egg, and milk until crumbly chunks of dough have formed. Drop the pieces into the soup to make small dumplings, cover, and simmer for 5 more minutes.

Makes 4 servings

CORNMEAL MUSH

Cornmeal mush is a hearty winter dish. Mary Riehl from Glick's recalls her mother making it. But there was a ritual: "Mom picked the corn. Dad dried the corn and ground it real fine before using it."

1 teaspoon salt	6 cups water
2½ cups yellow cornmeal	Flour, for dredging
2 cups cold water	Oil, for frying

Combine the salt and cornmeal in a large bowl, pour in the cold water, and whisk until well blended and smooth.

In a large saucepan, bring the 6 cups of water to a boil. Slowly whisk in the cornmeal mixture. Reduce heat to a simmer and stir until all lumps are dissolved. Continue cooking at a simmer for about 1 hour, stirring every 10 minutes.

Grease a standard loaf pan, pour in the cornmeal, and let cool. Cut into ½-inch slices, and dredge them lightly in flour. Cover just the bottom of a medium skillet with oil, heat the oil, and fry the cornmeal slices for about 5 minutes per side, or until lightly browned and crisp on both sides. Serve hot.

Makes 6 servings

HATFIELD FARMS OLD-FASHIONED APPLE DUMPLINGS

Barbara Esh gave us this recipe, an especially wonderful dessert during the winter.

2 cups brown sugar

2 cups water

$1/_4$ teaspoon cinnamon

$1/_4$ pound (1 stick) butter

2 cups flour

$2^1/_2$ teaspoons baking powder

$1/_2$ teaspoon salt

$2/_3$ cup shortening

$1/_2$ cup whole milk

6 medium Rome apples, pared and cored but left whole

Cream or hot milk, for serving

Preheat oven to 350° F. Grease a jellyroll pan. In a saucepan, combine the brown sugar, water, and cinnamon. Cook for 5 minutes, and add the butter.

In a bowl, sift together the flour, baking powder, and salt. Cut in the shortening. Gradually pour in the milk and mix lightly until the dough just holds together. Roll out the dough, and cut into 6 squares, each large enough to fully cover an apple. Place an apple on each square, and fill the cavity of each apple with some of the sauce. Pat the dough around the apple to cover completely, making sure the dough is sealed on top.

Place the dumplings 1 inch apart on the prepared baking dish. Pour the remaining sauce over the dumplings, and bake for 45 to 50 minutes, until the pastry is lightly golden. Serve in a bowl with hot milk or cream.

Makes 6 servings

AMISH CINNAMON FLOP

This dish was usually prepared during the fall and winter months to hold the family until supper, according to Rebecca Fay from Glick's. "Flop" describes a dish – like this one – that is flat.

12 tablespoons ($1\frac{1}{2}$ sticks) butter

1 cup sugar

2 cups plus 1 tablespoon all-purpose flour

$\frac{1}{4}$ teaspoon baking powder

Pinch of salt

1 cup milk

2 cups brown sugar

1 tablespoon cinnamon

1 tablespoon nutmeg

Preheat oven to 350° F. Grease two 8-inch round cake pans. In a large bowl, cream together 1 tablespoon of the butter with the sugar. In another bowl, combine the 2 cups of flour, baking powder, and salt. To the creamed butter and sugar, alternately add the flour mixture and the milk, stirring after each addition until smooth. Pour into the prepared cake pans, and lightly sprinkle the tops with the remaining 1 tablespoon of flour and 2 cups of brown sugar. Cut the remaining butter into small pieces and push them down into the batter. Sprinkle both tops with the cinnamon and nutmeg. Bake for 20 minutes, or until a tester inserted in the center comes out clean. Serve warm.

Makes 6 to 8 servings

DRIED SCHNITZ PIE

Dried apples have a concentrated flavor. Like all dried fruits, they need to be reconstituted before they can be used in any recipe. This recipe comes from Michelle Fetter from Glick's.

Pastry for 2 9-inch pie crusts	$1/4$ cup molasses
3 cups sliced dried apple pieces	$1/2$ teaspoon ground cloves
$1 1/2$ cups water	$1/2$ teaspoon ground cinnamon
$1/3$ cup sugar	

Preheat oven to 350° F. Place dried apple pieces in a medium saucepan, add the water, cover, and simmer until soft, about 10 minutes. Drain in a colander, pressing apples gently to remove as much water as possible. Add sugar, molasses, cloves, and cinnamon to the apples. Place one piece of the pastry in a 9-inch pie plate, place the apple mixture on the pastry, and cover with the second piece of pastry. Press edges to seal, use a fork to poke several holes in the top pastry, and bake for 30 to 35 minutes, until top crust is nicely browned. Serve warm or hot.

Makes 1 9-inch pie

CHAPTER 8 .... *The Specialty Merchants*

Reading Terminal Market is not just a place to eat or buy food. It's also home to distinctive shops selling cooking supplies, unusual equipment and gadgets, cookbooks, and other accessories. The merchants dealing in nonfood items also include local artisans selling jewelry and clothing.

Cookware is a natural for Reading Terminal Market, and if you enter from the Arch Street side, it's the first thing you'll see – cookware items on display from one of the market's newer stores, Foster's Gourmet Cookware. Foster's opened in the market in November 1995. Owner Ken Foster carries commercial-quality cookware, professional baking equipment, dishes, glassware, and many well-designed kitchen gadgets. One of his specialties is a diverse collection of peppermills.

Although most people probably don't think of flowers as edible, some of them are quite tasty. But any dinner table will look nicer with flowers – edible or not. Reading Terminal Market has three flower shops – Miriam's Market Flowers, The Flower Basket, and Flowers and Things.

The Cookbook Stall is also a natural for the market. In the early 1980s, Nancy and Edward Marcus published a cookbook, now out of print, titled *Forbidden Fruits and Forgotten Vegetables*. "This project left me heavily entrenched in cookbooks," Nancy recalled, "and led to the idea to open a cookbook store in the Reading Terminal Market." She fulfilled her dream in 1983, during the market's "renaissance," and opened her store, which carries a broad range of titles – health-oriented and vegetarian books, subjects from soups to salsas, bread baking to desserts, and a large selection of international and regional books. "The fun and challenge of a specialized bookstore," she said, "is getting those hard-to-find titles and subjects."

Across the way from The Cookbook Stall is Amy's Place, owned by Amy Podolsky. This charming store offers a wide selection of tableware, linens, and gifts. Handcrafted wooden serving pieces, fitted with radish, onion, or artichoke handles, as well as colorful ceramic bowls, vases, and jugs make this a perfect place for browsing. Her shop represents manufacturers and artisans from the Philadelphia region and around the world.

A stroll around the market will bring you to other interesting stalls that have no connection to food. Miscellaneous Libri, a stall concentrating on new and used books covering an immense range of subjects, is one of the most popular. Out of Africa, South American Imports, Viva Imports, Weinstones, Amazulu, and Natural Connections are other nonfood merchants, selling crafts, clothing, and items for the discerning shopper.

And finally, against the backdrop of a mural portraying the signing of the Declaration of Independence, is Johnnie Moore, Reading Terminal Market's Shoe Doctor, where Philadelphians for many years have come to have their shoes shined.

SWISS CHARD DIP

Swiss chard comes in two varieties, green and red, both of which have a similar taste. Trim off any tough ribs on large leaves, and chop them before using. This recipe comes from Nancy Marcus, owner of The Cookbook Stall, and appeared in her cookbook.

2 pounds Swiss chard, leaves only, well washed and coarsely chopped

1 large onion, finely chopped

1 clove garlic, minced

$\frac{1}{2}$ teaspoon dried red pepper flakes

$\frac{1}{3}$ cup olive oil

$\frac{1}{4}$ teaspoon salt

Juice of $\frac{1}{2}$ lemon

Pita bread, cut into wedges

In a large saucepan, combine the chard, onion, garlic, pepper flakes, and olive oil. Cook, covered, over medium heat for about 20 minutes, stirring occasionally until leaves are wilted. Reduce heat and continue cooking, covered, for about 1 hour, stirring occasionally, until chard becomes a thick, green mass.

Transfer to a serving bowl. Sprinkle with salt and lemon juice and allow to cool. Serve at room temperature with pita bread.

Makes 6 servings

PEPPER APPLE PIE

Betty Kaplan works at The Cookbook Stall and is a keen shopper at the market, too. She found the original recipe for a pepper apple cake attached to a jar of green peppercorns. Intrigued by the recipe, she set out to experiment and came up with this unusual pie. Green peppercorns have a clean, fresh, mild taste and are found bottled or in cans.

2 cups all-purpose flour

1/2 teaspoon salt

3/4 cup vegetable shortening

5 tablespoons cold water

1 tablespoon white vinegar

1 heaping teaspoon crushed green peppercorns

2 tablespoons butter, melted

4 to 5 tart apples, depending on size, peeled, cored, and thinly sliced

1/2 cup sugar

1 tablespoon lemon juice

In a bowl, sift together the flour and salt, cut in the shortening until it resembles coarse crumbs, and gradually add the cold water and vinegar until a soft dough forms. Divide the dough into two balls and refrigerate until needed.

Preheat oven to 450° F. In a small saucepan, melt the butter and add the crushed peppercorns. Place the apples, butter mixture, and sugar in a large bowl, and toss until well mixed. Sprinkle with lemon juice.

Roll out one of the balls of dough, and place it in a 10-inch pie plate. Pour the apple mixture over the dough. Roll out the other dough ball, place it on top of the apples, and crimp the edges to seal. Pierce dough with a fork in several places to allow the steam to vent during cooking. Sprinkle a little additional sugar on top, and bake in preheated oven for 10 minutes. Reduce heat to 350° F. and cook for 40 minutes, or until the crust is lightly golden.

Makes 6 servings

ROSE GERANIUM POUND CAKE

Rose geranium leaves are available in the spring. This cake was made by Cheryl Elliott of Flowers and Things for sampling at one of the market's herb festivals. It may seem that the geraniums don't do much, since they are discarded early in the recipe. But they do impart a distinct flavor to the butter and, ultimately, the cake.

12 rose geranium leaves

$1/2$ pound (2 sticks) butter

3 eggs, separated

1 cup sugar

$1^3/_4$ cups all-purpose flour

$1/_3$ cup half and half

1 teaspoon vanilla extract

Firmly press 6 of the geranium leaves around each stick of butter. Wrap in plastic wrap and refrigerate overnight.

Preheat oven to 300° F. Unwrap butter, and remove and discard geranium leaves. Let the butter soften at room temperature for 30 minutes. Bring the eggs to room temperature at the same time.

In a large mixing bowl, cream the butter, gradually adding $1/_2$ cup of the sugar. Beat until light and fluffy, and add egg yolks one at a time, beating well after adding each. Alternately add flour and half and half. Stir in vanilla.

With the egg whites at room temperature, beat them until soft peaks form. Add remaining $1/_2$ cup of sugar, 1 tablespoon at a time, beating until stiff peaks form. Stir about 1 cup of this mixture into batter. Gently fold in the remaining egg-white mixture. Pour batter into a greased 8- or 9-inch tube pan. Bake for 45 to 60 minutes, or until a cake tester comes out clean. Cool in pan for 15 minutes, remove, and cool completely before serving.

Makes 8 servings

LAVENDER JELLY

Jams and jellies can be made with a variety of herbs and herb flowers. The pungency of using different herbs with sweets such as jams and honeys is always a surprise but adds a delectable flavor to many dishes. This recipe comes from Flowers and Things.

$2^{1}/_{4}$ cups bottled apple juice

1 cup lavender flowers

$3^{1}/_{2}$ cups sugar

4 ounces ($^{1}/_{2}$ bottle) liquid pectin

5 sprigs lavender

Place apple juice and lavender flowers in a saucepan, and bring to a boil. Cover and remove from heat. Let stand for 15 minutes, then strain into a bowl.

Return 2 cups of the juice mixture to the saucepan, add the sugar, and bring to a full boil, stirring constantly. Stir in the liquid pectin and bring to a rolling boil for 1 minute, stirring constantly. Remove from heat. Skim off foam.

Place a sprig of lavender in each of 4 or 5 half-pint jars, and pour jelly into the jars within $^{1}/_{4}$ inch of the top. Immediately screw on the lids and place the jars in a hot water bath for 5 to 10 minutes, or according to manufacturer's directions. Jelly kept in jars without a top should be covered with a thin layer of paraffin. Proceed as above, but omit the hot water bath. Cover jars with a clean towel, let jelly cool, melt paraffin and pour over cooled jelly, let paraffin set, and cover with an attractive top.

Makes enough to fill 4 to 5 half-pint jars

MARIGOLD MUFFINS

Flowers and Things also supplied this recipe. Dry marigold petals by hanging bunches in a dark, airy, dry place. Darkness helps them retain their color.

$^3/_4$ cup milk

$1^1/_2$ tablespoons crushed dried marigold petals

3 tablespoons vegetable oil

$^1/_4$ cup honey

1 egg

2 cups all-purpose flour

1 tablespoon baking powder

$^1/_2$ teaspoon salt

Preheat oven to 400° F. In a saucepan, bring the milk to a boil, and add the crushed marigold petals and oil. Remove from the heat, strain into a bowl, discard marigold petals, and let cool to room temperature. Add the honey and egg, and mix to combine. In another bowl, sift together the flour, baking powder, and salt, and stir in the milk mixture. Mix just until combined.

Fill the cups of a standard muffin tin about two-thirds full and bake for 20 minutes, or until a tester inserted in a muffin comes out dry. Cool on a rack for 15 minutes and remove muffins from tin.

Makes 12 muffins

CHILI

Amy Podolsky from Amy's Place likes to prepare this version of chili for gatherings of friends during the cold winter months.

$^1/_3$ cup olive oil

1 large onion, coarsely chopped

1 pound sweet Italian sausage, meat removed from casing

1 pound ground beef

2 tablespoons tomato paste

3 cloves garlic, minced

2 teaspoons ground cumin

2 tablespoons chili powder

1 tablespoon Dijon mustard

2 teaspoons dried oregano

1 teaspoon salt

1 teaspoon black pepper

1 35-ounce can Italian plum tomatoes

$^1/_3$ cup red wine

$^1/_3$ cup chopped Italian (flat-leaf) parsley

1 16-ounce can kidney beans

1 cup pitted black olives

Heat oil over low heat in a large saucepan. Add onion and cook, covered, until soft and translucent, about 5 to 8 minutes. Break the sausage meat and ground beef into the saucepan, and cook over medium heat until well browned. Drain any excess fat.

Stir in tomato paste, garlic, cumin, chili powder, mustard, oregano, salt, and pepper. Add the tomato, wine, parsley, and drained beans. Stir well and simmer, uncovered, about 30 minutes. Taste for seasoning. Add olives, simmer through an additional 5 minutes, and serve.

Makes 6 to 8 servings

FOSTER'S COEUR À LA CRÈME

This recipe, the perfect Valentine's Day or spring dessert, using fresh dairy products and berries from the market, comes from Ken Foster of Foster's Cookware. It requires a special ceramic mold with holes in the bottom to allow the whey to drain from the cheeses. What remains will have a thick, creamy texture.

8 ounces cream cheese, softened

8 ounces cottage cheese

1 tablespoon sugar

Pinch of salt

$3/4$ cup heavy cream

1 pint strawberries or raspberries

Additional sugar to taste

Combine and beat the cream cheese, cottage cheese, sugar, and salt. Gradually add the cream and continue beating until smooth.

Line a heart-shaped ceramic mold with holes in the bottom with a couple layers of damp cheesecloth, allowing it to drape over the sides of the mold. Spoon the cheese mixture into the mold, smooth the top, and cover with the overhanging cloth. Place the mold in a shallow dish, and allow to drain overnight in the refrigerator.

To serve, slightly crush some of the berries and sweeten to taste. Unmold the cheese, arrange on a plate, garnish with whole berries, and serve with the crushed berries.

Makes 4 servings

Mail Order Merchants

Braverman's Bakery—215-592-0855
For Special Party Orders call Diane Braverman—215-232-7772

Termini Brothers Bakery–1-800-882-7650
Cookies

Harry G. Ochs & Sons—215-922-0303
Prime meats

L. Halteman & Sons Meats—215-925-3206
Smoked products, hams, sausages

Famous 4th Street Cookie Co.—215-629-5990
Cookies

Old City Coffee—215-592-1897
Variety of coffees

Pennsylvania General Store—1-800-545-4891
(call for catalog)
Pennsylvania food items and gift baskets

12th Street Cantina—215-625-0321
Mexican groceries

Amy's Place—215-922-4955
Tableware and kitchen gift items

The Cookbook Stall—215-923-3170
Cookbooks

Chocolates By Mueller—215-922-6164
Gourmet chocolates and candies

Tea Leaf—215-629-0988
Variety of teas and herbal teas

Foster's Gourmet Cookware—215-925-0950
Commercial-quality cookware

Iovine Brothers Produce—215-928-4366
Dried wild mushrooms and fruits

Index

181

The Frog Commissary Cookbook
Steven Poses, Anne Clark, and Becky Roller

"Lighthearted, full of ideas. . .Could inject new life into your dining and entertaining style."
Bon Appétit

The Original Philadelphia Neighborhood Cookbook
Irina Smith & Ann Hazan

"Now, in one book, some of the best home cooking in Philadelphia."
Jim Quinn in *Philadelphia Inquirer Magazine*

The Original Baltimore Neighborhood Cookbook
Irina Smith & Ann Hazan

Baltimore, like Philadelphia, is a city of neighborhoods. Now you can create over 250 recipes from more than 50 Baltimore neighborhoods.

If you cannot find a copy of these books at your local bookstore, they can be ordered directly from the publisher.

CAMINO BOOKS, INC.
P.O. Box 59026
Philadelphia, PA 19102

___ *Frog Commissary Cookbook* $19.95

___ *Original Philadelphia Neighborhood Cookbook* $16.95

___ *Original Baltimore Neighborhood Cookbook* $14.95

___ *Reading Terminal Market Cookbook* $16.95

Name_____

Address_____

City/State/Zip_____

All orders must be prepaid. Your satisfaction is guaranteed. You may return the books for a full refund. Please add $5.95 for postage and handling.

www.caminobooks.com